DEVOTIONAL REA

Listening in the Morning

TREVOR LLOYD

Copyright © Trevor Lloyd 2022

The author assumes full responsibility for the accuracy of all facts and quotations cited in this book.

Unless otherwise indicated, all Bible quotations are taken from the *New Revised Standard Version Bible*, copyright © 1989 the Division of Christian Education of the National Council of the Churches of Christ in the United States of America. Used by permission. All rights reserved.

Bible quotations marked "NIV" are from the *Holy Bible, New International Version*®, NIV® Copyright ©1973, 1978, 1984, 2011 by Biblica, Inc.® Used by permission. All rights reserved worldwide.

Bible quotations marked "KJV" are from the Holy Bible, King James Version.

Proudly published and printed in Australia by
Signs Publishing
Warburton, Victoria.

This book was
Edited by Lauren Webb
Proofread by Nathan Brown
Cover design by Shane Winfield
Typeset in Berkeley Book 11.5/15 pt

ISBN (print edition) 978 1 922373 67 0
ISBN (ebook edition) 978 1 922373 68 7

Contents

Foreword

I remember sitting in Avondale College Education classes listening to the deep voice of Dr Trevor Lloyd and being captivated by his astute selection of phrase. I was not your typical first-year Education student, having already completed a theology degree. But I found his reflections and deep spirituality insightful as he endeavoured to inspire the next generation of educators.

Dr Carol Tasker, then the South Pacific Division education director, asked Dr Lloyd, in his retirement, to consider writing a devotional book for our teachers—a task that he embraced with enthusiasm. The audience was diverse. Many with English as their second language. Some with postgraduate degrees. Some who have been content with one teaching qualification. But all have a focus and influence on kingdom growth and personal spirituality.

This book is the culmination of many hours of dedicated reading and writing. I am aware of the numerous emails sent and books that Dr Lloyd has read to gather the stories, to reflect on the applications and to make this such a practical resource. With this format, any school worship gathering will be enriched beyond measure.

I commend this book to you as one of the most valuable staff-room resources that Adventist Education could provide. As you each commence the working day with staff worship, take the time to read, ponder and discuss. Grow in your own personal faith journey as you listen in the morning and be refreshed for the day.

In this the 150th anniversary year of Adventist Education, this book is a fitting tribute to teachers past and present. It conveys a deep respect for God's workings down through the years. It provides a glimpse of the values and impact of Adventist Education. My prayer is that each teacher will be God-filled and student-focused as they continue to be blessed by indeed *Listening in the Morning*.

David McClintock, Director of Adventist Education, South Pacific Division

Dedication

To Ellen

Introduction

A recent tally has indicated that the Seventh-day Adventist Church has more than 9000 centres of learning globally, with enrolments coming in at more than two million.[1] Our challenge now, in an age of crisis, is to maintain the faithful witness of 150 years of Bible-based Adventist teaching and learning.

This collection of devotional readings is dedicated to this end. It is prepared with the staff of Adventist schools, colleges and universities in mind. If, as never before, we can see ourselves as vital parts of the "rightly trained" army long held before us, we may yet see this planet set aflame for God.[2]

The title *Listening in the Morning* has not been chosen lightly. As the gospel prophet wrote thousands of years ago, there is a special wakening at the commencement of each day to which teachers are especially called:

> The Lord God has given me the tongue of a teacher, that I may know how to sustain the weary with a word. *Morning by morning he wakens—wakens my ear* to listen as those who are taught (Isaiah 50:4).

We cannot help but notice that this special wakening of the ear is to be carried out by God Himself. If, as teachers, our tongues are to be truly effective in speaking to "sustain the weary," we—first of all—are to be learners. The passage tells us that God is waiting, "morning by morning" to waken and teach us, if we will listen.

Each day's reading opens with one or more passages from Scripture or the writings of Ellen White. The application of these passages to our work, day-to-day needs and spiritual lives as teachers is usually explored with a story and a question for reflection and discussion.

The book can be used for personal devotional reading but it was written with staff worship and group reflection in mind. In a school staff situation, the group might prefer to hear the topic presented by the worship leader from notes, rather than read word by word from the worship book.

At times, a particular topic might extend over two or more worship sessions, as staff are given opportunity to reflect on the topic and discuss ways they have been prompted to think along fresh lines.

The readings do not need to be read in order, though some days do continue the theme of the previous day's reading. Rather, topics may be selected for their special relevance to what is happening at a particular time in the school's schedule.

Wherever you may be as a reader, and whether you are alone or with other staff, my thoughts are with you day by day, as together we work and pray for the role our school system is to play during Earth's final days.

Trevor Lloyd
Turramurra, NSW, Australia
April, 2022

---

1 Statistics, as at December 31, 2019, for primary through to tertiary, and for schools, teachers and students are available at "Seventh-day Adventist Education, Education Department" <https://www.adventist.education/education-statistics>. The actual total given for schools is 9489 and for students is 2,044,709.

2 Ellen G White, *Education* (Mountain View, CA: Pacific Press Publishing Association, 1903), page 271.

Thinking higher and wider

"Go therefore and make disciples of all nations…teaching them to obey everything that I have commanded you. And remember, I am with you always, to the end of the age" (Matthew 28:19, 20).

In the year 1666, there was a great fire in the city of London. Thirteen thousand homes burnt down, along with 80 churches, including old St Paul's Cathedral. A new cathedral was needed and designing it was a job for the best architect that could be found.

The work was given to Sir Christopher Wren and he drafted a plan for a beautiful new church. Together with the dome, the building was to rise 111 metres (364 feet) above street level. The site was cleared, stone blocks were brought in and the stonemasons were set to work.

Sometimes, Sir Christopher would come by to check on progress. One day, he came without warning and set out incognito to meet some of the workers. Standing beside one man, he quietly asked, "What are you doing?" Not knowing to whom he was speaking, the worker replied, "I'm trimming this stone with a hammer and chisel."

Moving on, Sir Christopher asked another worker the same question and was told, "I'm earning money to support my family."

A third time, the famous architect put the question, "What are you doing?" and was told, "I'm helping Sir Christopher to build a cathedral."[1]

All three answers were worthwhile. And each answer tells us something about the one who gave it. Workers can have their eyes on what they are doing right now. Others may have a longer-term goal. Or they can look higher and wider and see something that helps them start the day with expectation and enthusiasm.

Suppose we were to come upon three teachers during school hours, out in the school yard, and ask, "What are you doing?" One might say, "I'm supervising the playground." Another might say, "I'm earning money to build a home of my own." Then another teacher might reply, "I'm getting to know these students so I can earn their trust and guide them towards a truly worthwhile future—in time and in eternity."

All these replies are important, of course. However, the third gives the grandest picture and the most exciting objective on which to focus.

Asking what we are doing here, in this very school and working for this very community, can be a reminder of the importance of putting into words a school mission statement—that is, the reason for our being here and what we are working towards. Such a statement cannot be formed overnight. If everyone takes part in sharing ideas about the mission statement, it can be owned by the whole school and can be a continual guide to where this school family wants to go.

---

1 Suzy Platt (editor), *Respectfully Quoted: A Dictionary of Quotations* (Washington, DC: Library of Congress, Congressional Reference Division, 1989), under alphabetic reference, Dreams. Attributed to Louise Bush-Brown, director of the Pennsylvania School of Horticulture for Women.

The school principal who listened in a new way

"Then the word of the Lord came to him, saying, 'What are you doing here, Elijah?'" (1 Kings 19:9).

The best of teachers and leaders can sometimes become discouraged. This was the experience of the prophet Elijah. One day, he was high up on Mount Carmel seeing fire fall from heaven, followed by black clouds and a rainstorm. A few days later, with Queen Jezebel vowing to kill him, he was lying alone in the desert under the shelter of a "solitary broom tree" (1 Kings 19:4). There he came to think he could do no more good and he asked for his life to be taken from him. Twice, however, an angel gave him food and water and he set out across the desert to "Horeb the mount of God" and hid there in a cave (1 Kings 19:8).

Elijah did not know it, but God still had work for him to do. Among those tasks was the responsibility of visiting the famous schools of the prophets for the last time as their principal.

But first, God had a lesson for this servant who felt so sorry for himself. And Horeb was the ideal place for it. It was where Moses saw the burning bush. It was where the Ten Commandments were given.[1] It was where the 12 tribes were terrified by thunder, lightning, fire, smoke and a great earthquake. It was the place where Israel became God's people and a nation.

In the morning, God came to the mouth of the cave where the prophet was hiding. The runaway heard an insistent voice asking, "What are you doing here, Elijah?"[2]

Elijah began to recite what he had tried so hard to do for God, and he finished up with what it had all come to, "[T]hey are seeking my life, to take it away" (1 Kings 19:10).

God replied, "Go out and stand on the mountain . . . for the Lord is about to pass by" (1 Kings 19:11). Then Elijah was given a reminder of the earlier days of Israel, when the nation camped in front of that very mountain. There was a strong wind that split the nearby mountains. There was an earthquake that shook Horeb to its core. There was a blazing fire. However, this time, the Lord was not in any of it.

Then there was something quite different. The prophet heard "a still small voice" (1 Kings 19:12, KJV)—"a gentle whisper" (NIV). This is a way that all of us can hear God—in the quietness of our hearts. I like to think that teaching-principal Elijah heard that whisper every day until he was taken by the fiery chariot to the heavenly courts (see 2 Kings 2:11). And we may do the same—until the sweet chariots of our day swing low to carry our students with us to our heavenly home.

Elijah was given mission assignments at a place of great importance to his spiritual family, and there he came to meet God in a fresh way—in a quiet, confiding whisper. What can we, as teachers, learn from this about not losing the legacy of those who went before us? What can we learn about staying connected to God? How can we apply these lessons to meet the challenges of each school day?

---

1 See Exodus 3 and 19.
2 The question is asked in 1 Kings 19:9, 13.

The gift in the heart

"See, the Lord has called by name Bezaleel...[a]nd he has inspired him [put in his heart, KJV] to teach" (Exodus 35:30, 34).

The 12 tribes of Israel were camped in their tents at the foot of Mount Sinai.[1] Their leader, Moses, went up onto the mountain to hear God's next assignment. He was told that a beautiful tabernacle—that is, a tent—was to be built and set up in the heart of their camp. An "industrial school" was to be organised and everyone would have the chance to join in, either giving some of their goods or working directly with their hands.[2] There would be carpentry, joinery, metalwork, weaving, sewing and embroidery. Gold would need to be beaten and shaped or cut and threaded. Jewels would need to be placed in beautiful settings. Tanning, dyeing, casting and moulding were all in the curriculum.

We aren't told how Moses felt about the prospect of a band of wanderers, a few weeks out of slavery, having to build a tabernacle. They knew how to make mud bricks, but how could they work in gold and silver and brass? And who could do the weaving and the embroidery?

God already had the answers. He had in mind a brilliant craftsman, who was right there in the camp—Bezaleel, from the tribe of Judah. And God had already given Bezaleel the gift of teaching. Notice that the gift was put in the most important place—in Bezaleel's heart. This meant that, while he taught, he could love his students and value them as persons.

When the gift of teaching is in someone's heart, they can see where their students are coming from and what they need next. They can guide them patiently step by step. And this might be the most wonderful thing: their students will want to be like their teacher—

and not just with the skills of mind and eye and hand. They will be drawn towards the teacher's values and goals. This process is called *identification*—and it is a secret not always well known to teachers.

The children and young people in our classes are struggling with what have been called *developmental tasks*. These tasks change as they get older. In early primary school, they may include sharing happily with others and getting along when playing games. In later primary years, children need to have greater mastery of reading, writing, mathematics and speaking. For teenagers, developmental tasks include relating naturally to other young people—both male and female—and settling on values that work in everyday life. As children develop, they look to adults they admire and emulate the way they manage these and other tasks. If that adult loves and respects them, they will tend to be loved and trusted in return and their values will be adopted.

Blessed is the school with teachers who, like Bezaleel, have been inspired to teach and have the gift of teaching in their hearts. Blessed is the home that has found a school like that—a place that can be trusted to teach from the heart to the hearts of its children and young people.

Head-gifted and hand-gifted teachers are important in a church-school setting—there is no place for low academic and handcraft standards. But what will show that this school has heart-gifted teachers as well? What are some values we hope our students will emulate as we get to know them and treat them with love and respect?

---

1 Also called Horeb, the Mount of God—the place where God spoke to Elijah.

2 See Ellen G White, *Education* (Mountain View, CA: Pacific Press Publishing Association, 1903), page 37.

An Adventist school leads the way

"The Lord will make you the head, and not the tail" (Deuteronomy 28:13).

"Seest thou a man diligent in his business? he shall stand before kings" (Proverbs 22:29, KJV).

In the 1920s, things on the islands of Mussau and Emira, in Papua New Guinea, were quite sad. A government anthropologist[1] wrote about it in his 1927 report, calling it a malaise. There was no particular disease—just a weariness of the body and mind. Housing was neglected and gardens were left to go wild. It seemed that people had lost the will to live.

Then there was a change. It happened when the Adventist mission came and brought teachers to help the people. They brought Naphtali from Fiji and set him to work on Emira, and they brought Oti from the Solomon Islands to work on Mussau with a European missionary and his family. A swamp was drained and the jungle was cleared. Now there was room for gardens, a house-lotu,[2] a schoolhouse, and housing for the staff and students. The villagers learned that God loved them and they followed their new teachers with joy and hope.

In the middle of these changes, another anthropologist arrived by boat to check things out. It was William Groves, who was not a missionary or an Adventist.[3] He never forgot the excited gathering of the whole population of Emira on the beach as his boat pulled in. He wrote: "[F]rom that moment of enthusiasm and joyous welcome, I knew that the 'Seventh-day mission' had these people . . . that here was no decadent people."

While on the island, Groves was invited to look over all the buildings and equipment. He was told that he could talk alone to the adults and children. From the start, Groves let the people know he wasn't a missionary or an Adventist. Then he tried all he could think of to test whether the people really wanted to follow the new way. He suggested other ways of living and made fun of what they were doing. He found that they "[stood] fast for the new life, with no regrets." As for the children, they already knew every organised game he introduced.

Groves was convinced of the importance of religion in meeting the needs of the people and was impressed with what he had seen. He remarked: "What a unique opportunity has the S.D.A. Mission at Mussau, starting in these days of educational enlightenment, to show all other organisations the way."[4]

Like the person described in Proverbs 22:29, the Adventist school leaders and teachers of those years had been diligent in their business and had indeed stood before "kings." What shall we do in our day? Now is our opportunity to show that Adventist schools are still ready to be the head and not the tail in making progress. Besides, since they are Christian schools, they can honour the name of Jesus, the greatest teacher the world has ever seen—and the Saviour of the world.

In the school work of this province, state or district, are there things crying out for a new demonstration of best practice—maybe things Adventist school supervisors wish they could see changed or things government education leaders want to see done better? Are we ready to take a lead in this school? With our Christian approach to guide us, are we prepared to develop thorough teaching programs, fresh teaching resources, and new and exciting methods?

---

1 In Greek, the word *anthropos* means "man" or "human beings." So then an an-thro-pol-o-jist is someone who studies about human beings—especially the way they have lived with each other in a variety of places and at other times.

2 A place for worship.

3 Later, when Papua New Guinea became independent from Australia, William Groves became the first government director of education.

4 This story and quotations it contains came from the following references:

W C Groves, "An anthropologist looks at the Seventh-day Adventist mission work in Mussau," Part 1, *Australasian Record*, August 20, 1934, pages 2, 3.

"Anthropologist's visit: Successful results achieved," *Squally Islands Mission*, August 23, 1934.

W C Groves, *Native Education and Culture Contact in New Guinea* (Melbourne: Melbourne University Press, 1936).

Being still

"Be still and know that I am God!" (Psalm 46:10).

Pastor Herbert Smith lived in southern California with his wife and their 10-year-old son.[1] Things were going well for Pastor Smith. He was happily married, he was a good preacher with a fine church, and his son was bright. He and his wife loved the boy dearly.

Then one evening, just before Christmas, something serious happened that Pastor Smith could not forget for the rest of his life. He was downstairs putting up some decorations when he heard some noise from the room above. Quickly, he hurried upstairs. There he found his boy kneeling at the foot of his bed and struggling for breath.

"Daddy," he gasped, "I can . . . hardly . . . breathe!"

As his wife held the boy to comfort him, Pastor Smith hurried to the phone to call the family doctor.[2] He discovered the doctor was not at home.

Another call. No answer! And another—still without success!

As panic was setting in, the pastor remembered a doctor that he knew some miles away in Hollywood. He told the distraught father to bring the boy to the phone. Then he asked several short questions: "Are his fingers turning blue and turning towards the palm of the hand? Skin yellowish in colour?"

"Yes. Yes. All of that."

"He has an oedema,[3] a swelling on the inside of the larynx. And it is starting to block the air supply to his lungs. An incision must be made in his windpipe to save his life. It is too far for me to come in time. Keep trying for a doctor near you."

Desperately, Pastor Smith had the operator try a hospital in a nearby town. "Too far to come in time to help," they told him.

As he stood with the receiver in his hand, two things flashed into his mind: the comfort he had tried to give to parents who had lost a child—and a Bible text from a sermon he had used at his church: "Be still and know that I am God."

Be still! At a time like that! Could he do it?

All right, he would do it. He hung up the receiver, paused, and cried: "Please, please, God, save my boy."

Just then, the phone rang. It was his doctor friend from Hollywood: "I've been trying to call you but your line has been busy. Not far from you there is a surgeon, visiting from overseas. Here is the address. Go and get him. He will know what to do."

The pastor found the doctor about to step off the front porch for an evening walk. "My boy!" the father exclaimed. "Oedema!"

The surgeon snatched up his bag and, a few minutes later, the boy was lying on the kitchen table, an opening was made in his windpipe and he could breathe freely again.

Have we been like that—with our "line" so busy that God is not able to reach us? Psalm 46:10 tells us what to do so that God can get through and let us know that He is God—the very One we need. God's children are to "be still" as they see Him working for them. Emily May (Grimes) Crawford (1864–1927) wrote about it in verse, putting it this way:

Speak, Lord, in the stillness,
While I wait on Thee;
Hushed my heart to listen
In expectancy.

If we were to take time to be still and listen to the promptings of God before we start to teach today, what results might our students notice? What difference might it make when dealing with challenging students?

---

1 This story is a real-life drama that happened in the first part of last century. It is adapted from Fulton Oursler, "Was it a lucky break?" in *Modern Parables* (Kingswood, Surrey: Cedar Book, 1955), pages 79–82.

2 In those days, most telephones were fixed to the wall with the receiver (that is, the ear-piece) hanging on an arm on one side. When you lifted the receiver, an operator at the telephone exchange would answer and find the number that you gave them.

3 The word is pronounced "uh-DEEM-uh."

Sons and daughters of the King

"Daughter…go in peace" (Luke 8:48).

During World War II, it was dangerous for many young people across Europe to stay in their homes, so some children from wealthy and titled families were taken to live in a castle in Switzerland until the war was over. Once their parents were not around to control them, many behaved badly in their classrooms and elsewhere. But not all. One of them kept about his studies and would not join in making trouble around the castle.

One day, the principal asked this young man why he behaved the way he did. He did not hesitate but replied, "You see, I am the son of a king."[1] And that was all he needed to say. He had a clear picture in his mind of who he was and of how princes behave, and he was not about to disgrace that picture.

This reminds me of a story Luke told about a suffering woman and a meeting she had with Jesus (see Luke 8:43–48.) Because she was bleeding, she was told she must not touch anyone around her. She must have felt rejected by humankind and, because of this, by God as well. Jesus was her only hope. Breaking the rules, she went on hands and knees in the crush and struggled towards Him as He was walking by.

At last, she had her chance and reached out between the shuffling feet around her. With the tips of her fingers, she touched the fringe of Jesus' robe. At once, two things happened. She knew she had been healed and Jesus knew that a miracle had taken place—for He noticed that power had gone out from Him.

She probably wanted to creep away quietly, but Jesus asked who had touched him. She came trembling and told her story. Then Jesus spoke to her directly—not to correct her or embarrass her but to encourage her. Gently, He said, "Daughter... go in peace," giving her a title she could carry forever in the sight of humans and of heaven. Now, if anyone asked who she was, she could say: "I am a daughter of a King—a heavenly King."

What are some ways we can show the young people we teach that God sees them as His sons and daughters—by letting them see that we value them that way ourselves?

---

1 The writer read this short anecdote in an Adventist publication (quite likely a journal) some years after World War II. With the account untraceable, it is here recounted from memory.

God takes a hand

"All your children shall be taught by the Lord, and great shall be the prosperity of your children" (Isaiah 54:13).

As teachers and parents, we are mentioned here in Isaiah 54. The text speaks of "All *your* children." We are in this verse because of the children. It is *they* who are at the centre of our work. It is *their* prosperity that we are aiming for. If there were no children given to us, we would be looking for another job.

Then comes some good news. In a church school or college, we are not teaching alone. We are told that our children shall be taught *by the Lord*. And this makes our schools quite different and special. The Lord Himself is at work in our classrooms, in our workshops and on our grounds, as the most important teacher. We are there to represent Him and make room for Him.

How does this happen? Before we go into the classroom, we ask God to go in with us and we know that He is with us by His Holy Spirit. Just by seeing and hearing us, the students will know that we have not come in alone that day. In a truly Christian classroom, God is speaking directly to the hearts and minds of our children and young people. They are being "taught by the Lord."

An experienced Adventist college professor put it like this: "Christian education and teaching begin with the teacher's own fellowship with Christ." And again:

> Christian education is not the student's hold upon certain ideas about God; it is God's hold upon the student and the teacher. . . . Our primary meaning and method are that something supernatural is happening to those young men and women in our classrooms, on our campuses, [and] in our dormitories.[1]

We should not be shy to ask for this, the greatest of gifts. Jesus has told us that our Father in heaven is more willing "to give the Holy Spirit to those who ask Him" than parents are willing to give food and gifts to their children (Luke 11:13).

At the beginning of each day, we may ask God for His Holy Spirit in our individual lives and as a school staff. We can pray that our words and actions will be fruitful for good and that they will leave space for God to reach our class members directly and personally. When this takes place, our text for today tells us that "the prosperity of [our] children" will be great.

Today's headline text was quoted by Jesus during His ministry on earth (see John 6:45). It promises a wonderful result that we, as Christian teachers, might treasure in our daily ministry—"Everyone who has heard the Father and learned from Him comes to Me."

What signs might students notice that convince them we have come into the classroom with God in our hearts and minds? Does our tone of voice when saying a student's name, or our facial expression when instructing or reproving, tell them they are of infinite worth to God?

---

1 Edward Heppenstall, "The adventure of learning and growing," *Journal of True Education*, Vol 13, No 5, June, 1951, pages 22–24.

Students who listen in a new way

"Speak, Lord, for your servant is listening" (1 Samuel 3:9).

The night he heard the Lord's voice was a great moment in the life of the boy Samuel. His teacher, Eli, was the high priest of Israel, and the words he encouraged his pupil to say are an example for all our children to follow.

Have students heard God in our classrooms and told Him they are listening? Perhaps in a whisper, they are opening their hearts and minds to the Spirit of God, and God Himself is speaking to them, carrying truth home to their hearts. This is a sign that we have a true church school and that our children are being "taught by the Lord."

How can we tell if this is happening in our classrooms? We can learn from the way Jesus taught. The members of His classes felt that He was speaking to them individually. He watched them as he taught and noticed when their faces lit up. He could see when the truth of what He was saying was reaching deep into their hearts.[1]

It is no surprise that the work of Christian teaching is an exciting adventure! It is "team teaching" at its most momentous. Jesus was looking for a meeting of heart and mind between the Spirit of God and His listeners. We too can make this our goal. God can give us eyes to read the faces of those who are hearing the whisper of God.

In what ways can we make provision for the young people in our classes to hear the whisper of God in their own hearts?

---

1 See Ellen G White, *Education* (Mountain View, CA: Pacific Press Publishing Association, 1903), page 231. She adds that when Jesus could see that "truth had reached the soul . . . there vibrated in His heart the answering chord of sympathetic joy."

Ears that hear the "inner voice"

"Take heart, son; your sins are forgiven" (Matthew 9:2).

Tom Brown was due to hand in an English assignment.[1] Because it was not finished, he quietly took it from his bag in a maths class, to add a few final words. Then the worst thing happened. Catching sight of what was happening, the maths teacher, Mr Benson, swept down, snatched up the essay and exclaimed: "Not in my classroom, you don't!" Then he rumpled it between his hands.

Tom gave a cry of resentment and mumbled a few words under his breath. At this, Mr Benson shouted, "What was that? To the principal!"

Long ago, there was a different kind of disturbance in a famous classroom. It was caused by four students taking the room apart. They were not trying to get out. Rather, they were trying to get in—and were determined to bring a handicapped friend to the attention of the Teacher.

Both Mark (2:1–12) and Matthew (9:2–8) tell the story. Carrying their friend with them, the four friends climbed the outside steps up to the roof of the classroom, then they started digging into the moss and earth on the roof. At last, they made an opening and lowered the invalid, still on his mat, down in front of the Teacher Himself.

Like all teachers in the middle of a lesson, this Teacher wanted to hold the attention of the class. With dust and bits of leaf floating around Him, did He say, "Not in my classroom, you don't!"? Not so!

This was no ordinary teacher. Everyone in the room, including a bunch of spying local teachers—the scribes—knew, or thought they knew, what the handicapped man on the mat most wanted. Jesus was a healer as well as a teacher, so they all waited for Him to perform a miracle.

However, Jesus did not at first say or do what they all expected. He could hear something no-one else could hear—the inner cry of this trembling man's heart. Those in the township had told the helpless man that his paralysis had been brought on by his sins. (Some of those *other* teachers there may themselves have spoken that way.)

The Teacher above all teachers looked intently at the invalid latecomer and with a smile of reassurance said, "Take heart, son." Then, in response to the pleading inner voice, He added, "Your sins are forgiven" (Matthew 9:2).

Shall we pray for the gift to hear that way? Anyone can reprove misbehaviour and interruptions, but it takes a special kind of teacher to hear a cry from the heart—and to speak in answer to that pleading inner voice.

What will it take for us to learn to hear the pleading inner voices of our students—especially the cries from the hearts of those who may be troublesome? What are some ways we can discover, in confidence, the special problems they are facing both at home and at school?

---

1 The present writer has lost track of the source of this anecdote. It was in an Australian education journal and appeared in the early 1960s. It is recounted here from memory.

New directions for broken lives

"Stand up, take your bed and go to your home" (Matthew 9:6).

I knew a teacher and principal of an Adventist school who must have understood well the story of the paralytic in Mark 2 and Matthew 9. A 14-year-old student was sent to him for starting a disturbance in the technical drawing class. The principal looked at him with understanding and the lad looked back and decided he could trust this man.

The principal asked quietly, "What is it, Malcolm?"[1]

After a short pause, the reply came back, "Sir . . . I can't do my maths."

That is not that the kind of answer we might expect to get from a boy who has just poked someone with the pointed end of a compass. Yet Malcolm's simple statement was a truthful plea from the heart: "I feel my future falling to pieces in front of my eyes. Please, please, can you help me?"

Do students trust us enough to share their problems with us? If they do, we are well placed to help them overcome their challenges and find confidence and purpose.

Jesus' last words to the paralytic in Mark 2 and Matthew 9 provided just this type of encouragement: "Stand up, take your bed and go to your home." The former paralytic was now to be on his feet—not on his back. He was no longer to be dependent on others to make his bed—he could carry it where he wished. He could now choose his own path.

This story can be part of our mission today. As Christian teachers we may teach maths or English or history or art, but most of all we help build and re-build lives. Teachers of subjects other than Bible can do things for our students that Bible teachers and school chaplains cannot do, and our work in imparting these skills should be second to none. When students are doing well in academic and practical subjects, they may be more relaxed and ready to listen to what we have to say about the values we are inviting them to accept. We can help our young people to go out with confidence to fulfil their purpose and make a difference in the lives of others struggling to find their place.

What other special opportunities do teachers of subjects other than Bible have? How can they play a special role in helping students who are struggling?

---

1 Not his real name.

Gentle gifts of the Servant Teacher

"Here is my servant, whom I have chosen, my beloved, with whom my soul is well pleased. I will put my Spirit upon him, and he will proclaim justice to the Gentiles. He will not wrangle or cry aloud, nor will anyone hear his voice in the streets" (Matthew 12:18, 19).

When I was a student in secondary school, my first two teachers were fine Christians and true Adventists. Both were in their 30s. Yet, the earlier teacher—a male—was the least effective teacher I ever had. In contrast, the later one—a female teacher—was the most effective teacher I ever had.

She was well-groomed, poised and neatly dressed. She spoke softly and meaningfully and caught my attention in all the subjects she taught—whether Bible, algebra or Latin. Thinking back now with my own professional training in mind, I realise that I identified with her closely—even to the extent of being attracted to the things she liked. She spoke in a relaxed way and her voice carried naturally and pleasantly—as if it had a smile at the back of it. Needless to say, I do not remember her losing control of herself or of the class, or ever raising her voice sharply.

You will understand why I think of her, the best teacher I ever had, when I read the above passage from Matthew which, in turn, is quoted from Isaiah 42:1, 2. It describes a servant who was chosen and loved by God. The Spirit of God was placed upon Him. He lived and spoke justly, and the justice that He lived was to go out to the wider world. Here was a teacher who would not "wrangle or cry aloud"—no noisy arguing or shouting. The passers-by on the nearby streets would not hear an angry voice through the walls and windows.

We can understand why Matthew saw Jesus as the perfect fulfilment of this ancient prophecy. Commenting on this passage, William Barclay notes: "In Jesus there is the quiet, strong serenity of one who seeks to conquer by love, and not by strife of words."[1]

What makes a lowered, steady, meaningful voice so authoritative and effective?

---

1 William Barclay, *The Gospel of Matthew*, Vol 2, Revised Edition (Philadelphia: The Westminster Press, 1975), page 34.

Not crushing but binding up

"He will not break a bruised reed or quench a smouldering wick[1] until he brings justice to victory" (Matthew 12:20).

Beyond the city of Perth, Western Australia, is a line of hills called the Darling Range. There you can find the twin valleys of Carmel and Bickley. Around the year 1900, an Adventist colporteur came into that region. A number of the farmers turned gladly to what they read in the books they bought from him, and they soon set up a lively church and a boarding school. It was first called the Darling Range School (in 1907) and today it is called Carmel Adventist College.

In the early 1930s, at the height of the Great Depression, a teenager came to the school from the inland gold-mining town of Kalgoorlie. He was a restless, golden-haired, slightly built young man by the name of Wilbur. From the start, anyone could see he would find it difficult to fit into dormitory life and follow the classwork. His fellow students suffered from his disturbances and so did the residence dean and the principal to whom he was sent more than once. How long could a young man without purpose and direction in his life be allowed to remain in the halls and classrooms?

Finally things came to a head. It appeared that he would need to be returned to his family in the goldfields of Western Australia. There was to be one further visit to the office of the principal.

We don't have details of what happened that day. It may be that the principal had recently read:

> Every true teacher will feel that should he err at all, it is better to err on the side of mercy than on the side of

> severity. . . . The true object of reproof is gained only when the wrongdoer himself is led to see his fault and his will is enlisted for its correction.[2]

What we do know is that the two of them spoke for a time and then knelt beside each other for prayer. The principal prayed from his heart over the wayward teenager, asking for God to intervene. Then the two of them stood to their feet and shook hands, and the young man went out—now with new goals and new resolve.

One of his fellow students told me, decades later, it was a "Damascus Road" conversion. Wilbur applied himself to his studies and finished his course successfully. In later years, he married his college English teacher. He was ordained as a church pastor and he and his wife, Maimie, became a successful evangelistic team.

One last occasion should be mentioned. While still in active service, Pastor Wilbur Stewart was in the city of Melbourne. There he heard that his former principal had lost his way spiritually and was laid up in a hospital bed. He determined to visit this man who earlier had not broken a bruised reed or snuffed out an offensive smouldering wick.

What followed was a sight to make the angels look on in wonder. The one-time wayward boy now stood by the bed and prayed over his former principal. Eternity alone can tell us the outcome of that prayer.

Still today, the "bruised reeds" will be found in our classrooms and dormitories. The "smouldering wicks" that offend the nostrils of the school staff will be sent to our offices. Here is our opportunity to cooperate with God's Spirit—not to break but to bind up, not to snuff out but, in partnership with God, to breathe back to life.

How much do we know about the actual struggles and temptations of the young people in our classes? The sooner we find out what "bruises" they are suffering from and what is causing their "wick of life" to smoulder, the sooner we can support and guide them.

1 In those early days, a reed was a wooden staff used, for example, by a shepherd in leading and protecting his flock. If it was bruised or splintered, it could damage the shepherd's hand. He might be tempted to put it across his knee, break it and throw it away. The alternative was to bind it up. In the simple labourers' homes of those days, the only indoors light might have come from a wick lying in a dish of oil. If it burnt poorly, it could smoulder and give off unpleasant smoke. The householder could either snuff it out or breathe on it to bring it back to burn brightly.

2 Ellen G White, *Education* (Mountain View, CA: Pacific Press Publishing Association, 1903), pages 294, 291.

"What is that in your hand?"

"So he threw the staff on the ground, and it became a snake" (Exodus 4:3).

Early one morning, a shepherd, with his staff in his hand, led his flock out into the wilderness. This day was to be one of the great hinge points of history, yet this shepherd knew nothing of it at first. Then, at a burning bush, God spoke directly to him and called him to lead Israel out of Egypt to the very mountain where they were then speaking.

As witness to the truth of his call, God gave Moses three signs. In this reading and the next, I want to look at two of these signs as illustrations of the way spiritual leaders (including us as teachers) are to understand their work.[1]

The first sign involved the staff Moses held—his instrument to protect and guide his flock. It represented the power that God gave to His servant for the huge task ahead. He was to shepherd an unruly bunch of former slaves as they became a nation dedicated to their Lord.

Early in his conversation with God, Moses was told to throw the staff to the ground. There, it changed: it was no longer an instrument of God-given authority and power for the guidance and protection of his flock. It had become a snake—a reminder of the selfishness that would try to take over his life when his "flock" tempted him to become impatient.

We know that Moses held that staff high month after month, year after year. Even when his people seemed about to stone him, this meekest man in all the earth would not turn against them and fight for his own reputation. Even when they turned to idolatry, he was willing to give himself in their place, offering to have his own name blotted out of God's book.

Just once in all that wilderness turmoil did the heaven-appointed shepherd allow the staff to "fall to the ground." When they didn't have water to drink, the people provoked Moses sorely. They even dared to say that it would have been well to have died when their "kindred died before the Lord!" (Numbers 20:3).

God told Moses what to do. Together with his brother, Aaron, Moses was to take the staff, go to the rock and command water to come from it. Blinded with impatience, frustration and anger, Moses cried out bitterly: "Listen, you rebels, shall we bring water for you out of this rock?" (Numbers 20:10). Then he raised the staff and struck the rock twice.[2]

As teachers we too are heaven-appointed authority figures. Like Moses, we will often be tempted to lash out in frustration when our students complain and misbehave and to feel the burden is ours to bear alone. But if, by God's grace, we maintain self-control, our students may be registering a number of important things about themselves—like "I matter to my teacher and my teacher loves God, so I must matter to God. My teacher matters to me—and God does, too."

For this present school day, with God at our side, the staff may be held high. And let's remember that all school days come one at a time.

Sometimes during the school day we are going to feel stressed. Impatience and frustration may rise up and threaten to boil over on our students. What are some helpful ways of managing these situations?

---

1 This reading and the next have been adapted from S H Hooke, *The Siege Perilous* (London: SCM Press, 1956), pages 225, 226.

2 For this misuse of authority, Moses looked upon the Promised Land but did not lead the people in. He died on Mount Nebo and was buried by heavenly hands (see Deuteronomy 34). Still dear in heaven's eyes, his burial site was visited by the archangel Michael (see Jude 9), and Moses was there with Elijah on the Mount of Transfiguration to encourage Jesus as He faced His final weeks before the cross (Matthew 17:1–3).

The plague within

"[W]hen he took it out, his hand was leprous" (Exodus 4:6).

The second of the three signs given to Moses becomes still more personal. The first was about the staff of authority. The next was about the hand that holds the staff—and about what motivates that hand.[1]

Still standing barefoot by the burning bush, Moses was told to put his hand "into his cloak." (I am assuming it was his right hand and he placed it over his heart.) Upon taking his hand out from under his cloak, he looked at it and discovered it was leprous and bleached "white as snow." So then, before taking on the leadership of an unruly bunch, he had better understand that hidden within his own bosom, waiting to express itself in his hand—and in his voice!—was the most dreaded of all diseases.

King Solomon knew about it. In his prayer of dedication of the temple, he recognised that those who call on God are to pray "knowing the *afflictions* of their own hearts" (1 Kings 8:38). The King James Version calls it the *plague* of their own hearts—a reminder that there is in the nature of humankind "a bent to evil, a force which, unaided, [we] cannot resist."[2]

What hope have we, as teachers, and our students with us, of standing up against this inner force? Ellen White gives us the secret:

> To withstand this force, to attain that ideal which in his inmost soul he accepts as alone worthy, he can find help in but one power. That power is Christ. Cooperation with that power is man's greatest need. In all educational effort should not this co-operation be the highest aim?[3]

We witness the power of that co-operation in the story of a pre-breakfast seminar Jesus held in a corner of the temple courtyard.[4] The scribes set out to disturb the class and catch the Teacher out by bringing in a woman "who had been caught in adultery." They forced her to stand in front of the class while they challenged Jesus to pass judgment on her. After dealing with the hypocritical accusers—more gently, we might say, than they deserved—Jesus told the woman that He did not condemn her. Then He said: "Go your way, and from now on do not sin again."

Here is something wonderful. If someone else said to me, "Don't go on in that way," it might make little difference. But suppose I have felt Jesus close to me and heard Him say that my sins are forgiven—that from that day I can start anew and we can walk the path ahead together. *That* makes all the difference. Now, the plague of the heart need not dictate the behaviour of the hand or the voice.

In practical terms, what might we do to come into a co-operative relationship with the divine power made available to us (see Ellen White, Education, *page 29)?*

---

1 As for the previous reading, this devotion is adapted from S H Hooke, *The Siege Perilous* (London: SCM Press, 1956), pages 225, 226.

2 Ellen G White, *Education* (Mountain View, CA: Pacific Press Publishing Association, 1903), page 29.

3 ibid.

4 See John 8:2–11.

Schools with moral power

"It is the degree of moral power pervading a school that is a test of its prosperity" (Ellen White, *Testimonies for the Church*, Volume 6, page 143).

What signs shall we look for in a church school that show we are succeeding? Around the turn of the last century, some Adventist school leaders were looking to attract students by playing down the things that are distinctive in our teachings. Religion was one of them. Christian standards in entertainment was another.

Ellen White raised her voice against such a practice, claiming:

> To lower the standard in order to secure popularity and an increase of numbers, and then to make this increase a cause of rejoicing, shows great blindness.[1]

It was in this context, that she wrote today's opening reading about the importance of moral power. She continued:

> It is the virtue, intelligence, and piety of the people composing our schools, not their numbers, that should be a source of joy and thankfulness.

What are the practical outcomes in a school with a true sense of moral power? Think of the way the students relate to each other—in the classroom, in the library, in the grounds. Do they respect each other whether or not teachers can see and hear them? Would bullying be seen as out of place? Is defence of the shy and timid seen as the normal and accepted practice? Is there a sense of encouragement of those struggling academically, rather than a sense of rivalry? When anyone—student or teacher—feels that one of the school family is coming across as disrespectful, do they feel free to say so calmly and directly?[2]

How about the attitude each student has towards themselves? Is there quiet self-respect? Do they regard cheating as not on? Is there a healthy attitude towards personal failure and personal success? Do they know that they matter to us for who they are rather than how well they do their schoolwork?

That sounds to me like moral power at an advanced level!

Staff may be interested to share instances of the way particular schools they have known have demonstrated moral power in the classroom, playground or elsewhere. Does the group have suggestions for ways in which such an attitude might be encouraged?

---

1 Ellen G White, *Testimonies for the Church*, Volume 6 (Mountain View: CA, Pacific Press Publishing Association, 1901), page 143.

2 A good Christian book on this subject is *Caring Enough to Confront* by David Augsburger (Baker Publishing Group, 2018).

Student power in and out of the classroom

"Students, you can make this school first class in success by being labourers together with your teachers to help other students.... Be determined that you will make this school a success, and if you will heed the instruction given in the word of God, you may go forth with a development of intellectual and moral power that will cause even angels to rejoice" (Ellen White, *Fundamentals of Christian Education*, pages 464, 465).

I once knew a 16-year-old who had stayed clear of cigarettes, alcohol and drugs thanks to his home influences and the Christian school he was attending. One of his classmates was particularly influential in his decision to stay on that path. One day, when they were talking one-to-one, the classmate said, "Drugs are out for me—I don't want to lose control of my life." At that moment, moral power in that school expressed itself through the power of quiet student leadership.

There is something here that we must not forget. Student power, for good or ill, is real. Some students have more of it than others, and they are the natural leaders. What they say and do has a lot of influence in a group. Sometimes the group may be small—perhaps three or four students only. Sometimes the group may be large—perhaps covering most of a class or more than one class.

How do these natural student leaders come to have this position of power? In every group, there are some things that matter most to the students themselves. They are the *group values*. As Christian teachers, we hope and work and pray for positive values to be held by each group. Positive values at school include things like working to do one's best and get the most out of the classes, and standing up for those who are struggling in the classroom and playground and encouraging them to have their say. At the same time, we would be disappointed to notice negative values such as showing one's toughness by going against the school rules and bullying those who are weaker and struggling.

Group values may be spoken about openly within the group or they may be unspoken but well accepted just the same. Whichever it is, members in a group who represent the group values best will be the group leader(s) and have the most influence and power. If positive values are held by a group and its natural leader(s), the school's program of character building is off to a flying start. If negative values are held by a group or any of its sub-groups, we have a serious barrier to our work of Christian education.

With God at our side, what steps may we take in building positive group values and discouraging negative group values? Several suggestions are outlined below—not necessarily in order of importance.

Maintaining student success in tests and examinations

There could be a number of reasons why students behave badly in class. If they have failed again and again in tests and examinations, they may have given up on achieving success in their classwork. Maybe there are others in the same situation, and they want to show each other that there are other ways of getting group approval. Sadly, this could include being rebellious, experimenting with drugs or bullying the weak.

Even if there are only a few classrooms where this sad situation has appeared, we can pray and work towards overcoming it. I suggest that as teachers we take personal responsibility for student results in tests and examinations. We are to find fresh ways of explaining difficult ideas. We can teach for success for all members of the class—the strugglers as well as the gifted. We can follow up results and make sure that extra teaching is given—best of all, by ourselves.

Subject matter that matches the real, personal needs of the age group

Students in every age group have special needs they are struggling to meet. These can be about getting along with the other members of the class by sharing and by accepting others even if they are different. Or they can be about finding out who they are as people with their own values, hopes, goals and employment prospects, and relating respectfully to the opposite sex. If the curriculum is arranged to help the student get answers to questions like these, then we are well off. If it is not so arranged, we could plan to make it so. If my class and this school are known to help with these answers, the student is likely to accept them in forming their group values.

Quiet identification by the students with the teacher

Students of all ages are looking for models on which they can base their lives and arrange their future. Some of them may choose a film star and some a sports star. What they are looking for is someone who seems to have made a success in planning their lives—with this showing in the way they dress, the way they relate to the students (some quiet humour can help), in the interests they choose and in the way they talk of them. If a teacher comes across as interesting and exciting and as finding lots of fun and satisfaction in life, students may well identify with that teacher and model their values in their own lives.

Classes where the teacher has become a role model for most of the students are not hard to pick. Notice the way the students watch their teacher with interest and maybe at least a half smile. Notice the way they are ready to laugh at even the beginning of a joke. Notice the way they take a close interest in descriptions the teacher gives of the way they faced and solved personal life problems.

Identifying social groups and group leaders

In view of the importance of student group leadership and moral power in a school, the school staff may be interested in discovering the natural groups operating in classrooms and the playground and those taking on leadership roles within those groups.

A start may be made by noting the spontaneous clusters in the playground and in free group work. Then there is a more serious approach that involves the drawing up of a "sociogram," that is, a map of student groups within the classroom. A natural way to work towards the preparation of a sociogram is to choose a class project that can be conducted by arranging the students into small groups.

Students can be invited to give their preference about group members and leaders by writing their own name at the top of a small sheet of paper and then listing four or five members of the class with whom they would like to work. They are also invited to underline the name of the one they would like to have leading their group.

The teacher's task is then to arrange the names of the students into clusters—maybe four or five for each group—with the choices connected by arrows. The groups can then meet, perhaps first settling the name of the group leader—then deciding which feature of the project interests them most. Examples of the way such sociogram maps may appear can be found by doing an internet search with the term "sociogram."

The findings of a sociogram may best be regarded as confidential between the individual student and the class teacher and, say, the school chaplain and the school principal.

How might knowledge of the findings of a sociogram be used to strengthen the sense of moral power within a school? Do you have any suggestions for guiding student power in positive directions? What might be done for encouraging loners—and what is better not done?

"To everyone their work"

"It's like a man going away: He leaves his house in charge of his servants, each with his assigned task, and tells the one at the door to keep watch" (Mark 13:34, NIV).

"Not more surely is the place prepared for us in the heavenly mansions than is the special place designated on earth where we are to work for God" (Ellen White, *Christ's Object Lessons*, page 326).

The prophet knew it was a dangerous mission. There was already a king on the throne, but God had told Samuel to go and anoint another.[1]

When he arrived at Bethlehem, the elders went out nervously to meet him. He quietened their fears by announcing a sacrifice and a feast. They were all invited to the home of Jesse.

Before the feast, Jesse brought in his sons, one at a time, so Samuel could meet them. This, the prophet thought, would be a quick assignment. Any one of these young men could wear the royal crown. Soon, seven of Jesse's sons had come by, but God had still not said, "That's the one." The feast could not start. The ox must stay on the spit a little longer.

"Have I seen all your sons?" Samuel asked.

"There *is* one other," Jesse admitted, "the youngest of all. But we gave him the job of keeping the sheep." He might have added, "I didn't think to call him. He watches the sheep and composes songs. What sort of future could he have?"

With a set look on his face, the prophet directed, "Send and get him now; we will not sit down until he is here."

So, David arrived home from the grassy slopes of Bethlehem, fresh-faced, upright, handsome and wondering what all the fuss was about. And God said, "That is the one. Anoint him."

Out in the fields day by day, with the works of God all around him and his lyre at his side, David had felt close to God.[2] Now, the Spirit of the Lord came upon him mightily from "that day forward" (1 Samuel 16:13).

What does this story mean for us as teachers—and for the children and young people we work with each day? Like the prophet Samuel, we cannot know their hearts or read their innermost thoughts, and we do not know what God has in mind for their future lives. As in the parable, God gives "to every man his work" (Mark 13:34, KJV), but He has not told us what that special work will be.

"God's plan of life has a place for every human being. Each is to improve [their] talents to the utmost."[3] And that is one reason why these young people have been entrusted to our care. If we educate them faithfully and lead them to listen to God's Spirit now, like David, they may have the Holy Spirit come upon them mightily as they accept God's "anointing" for the special work known—as yet—only to God.

May God guard us from limiting what that place might be and help us to encourage the talents that are evident now, while looking for other gifts that may presently lie hidden from view.

In what ways is vocational guidance in church schools likely to be special? In what school grades might it commence? What principles might it best follow?

---

1 The story is told in 1 Samuel 16.

2 See Ellen G White, *Education* (Mountain View, CA: Pacific Press Publishing Association, 1903), page 164: "Through song, David...held communion with heaven."

3 ibid, page 226.

In the service of the Servant-King

"[T]he Son of Man came not to be served but to serve" (Matthew 20:28).

Some lessons, it seems, are especially hard to learn. Jesus and His disciples were on their last journey to Jerusalem. At that time, the mother of James and John asked Jesus for the top positions in the coming kingdom to be given to her two sons. When the other disciples heard of this, they were angry.

In the face of this envy, bitterness and rivalry, Jesus called the group to Him. He wanted them to know how leaders in His cause should go about leading. He explained it this way:

> You know that the rulers of the Gentiles lord it over them, and their great ones are tyrants over them. It will not be so among you; but whoever wishes to be great among you must be your servant, and whoever wishes to be first among you must be your slave; just as the Son of Man came not to be served but to serve, and to give his life a ransom for many (Matthew 20:25–28).

Soon they were in the Upper Room. Now there was opportunity to show they understood what Jesus had explained to them those days before. And they failed. There, at the Passover supper, they looked around and noticed there was no slave ready to wash their sandalled feet. No-one moved.

Then, something happened for the first time in history. The King stood to His feet. He made His way to the side of the room where the implements of the slave were waiting. There, He wrapped a towel around His waist and poured water into a bowl.

The Twelve looked on in wonder as their Lord walked back to the group. Would He pass the bowl to one of them? He did not. Instead, He placed it beside the feet of one of them. Then, kneeling, He untied the sandal thongs and lifted the dust-stained feet into the bowl.

As the Master moved around the circle, His touch was not thoughtless and uncaring. Rather, it was gentle and tender and spoke of love. In that moment, it electrified Judas, the betrayer. Jesus' touch was saying, "How can I give you up?" Right then, Judas knew that he was loved and his heart prompted him to embrace his rightful Lord and confess the evil of his plans. But then he hardened his heart. He might have said within, "If Jesus is Master of this group and He kneels like this before His subjects, I can expect nothing better. This is not for me." He silenced the appeal of the Holy Spirit for the last time. No-one is beyond hope, except those who refuse the call of love.

For the other disciples in the room, things went differently. The same sunshine that hardens clay will melt wax. They said within, "Jesus is my Lord and Master—and I love Him. If He takes the place of the servant, then I shall do the same." Now they were not struggling against each other. Now they were loving fellow servants of the Servant-King—the greatest vocation we can ever know.

As a teacher who takes the name of Jesus, do I stand in the ranks of the Servant-King? Then I am ready to motivate my students in this same cause.

What might we put in place in our classrooms that will encourage support and cooperation among our students, rather than rivalry?

"No-one cared for my soul"

"Look on my right hand and see—there is no-one who takes notice of me; no refuge remains to me; no-one cares for me" (Psalm 142:4).

James Baldwin (1924–1987) was brought up in Harlem, New York, the son of a one-time African-American slave. Early in life, he started to write and he did it well. But he was not settled in his mind about just who he was. At that time, there were struggles over whether Black children could attend the same schools as the white. He felt cut off from both the white population and the Black.[1] So he decided to go to Paris to try to work things out. It was easier there in some ways. Later, he returned to America—to Harlem, then to the Southern states.

Baldwin wanted to find peace with himself. Often, he felt lonely—so lonely that when he wrote about it, he called the book *Nobody Knows My Name*. That would be a sad way for anyone to live. We begin to know who we are by the way other people relate to us—especially those who are important to us. These are people who know our names, our interests and our hopes. They care about our plans and they talk to us about them from day to day.

But not everyone has it that way. At one time, the future King David was hiding in a cave in fear of losing his life. He wrote, "there is no-one who takes notice of me . . . no-one cares for me." Could that be the experience of any of the children and young people in our classrooms and playgrounds?

There are teachers with a special gift for quietly finding out the interests of those within their reach. There are even teachers who are able to bring lonely students within reach of other students with similar interests. Before, they may have been like David who felt that "no refuge remains for me." But now they see our classrooms as "cities of refuge."

The King James Version translates the last line of our verse for today as: "no-one cared for my soul." Today, one of us may be given an opening for remedying that situation for just one pupil. Perhaps there is a student in one of our classes who has gone through the day without hearing their name said with interest and excitement. Perhaps no-one else might have asked about something they mentioned the day before. As teachers, we need God-given understanding and empathy to be a loving refuge for students who are crying inside for someone to care about them.

May it never be said of the students in our classrooms that they had to go somewhere else, perhaps to a harmful environment, to find someone who would listen—someone who would use their name gently with a smile and with understanding.

What signs (for example, facial expressions, words, behaviours) might tell us which students in our classes are lonely and looking for someone to love them?

---

1 See James Baldwin, *Nobody Knows My Name: More Notes of a Native Son* (London: Michael Joseph, Ltd, 1961), pages 17–23, 89, 92.

As those who must give account

"Obey them that rule over you, and submit yourselves: for they watch for your souls, as they that must give account" (Hebrews 13:17, KJV).

"See, I and the children whom the Lord has given me are signs and portents in Israel from the Lord of hosts" (Isaiah 8:18).

Gladys Aylward (1902–1970) was born in London, England. From an early age, she believed that God wanted her to be a missionary in China. However, when she approached the China Inland Mission, they told her she was too old to learn the Chinese Mandarin language.

Very well, she decided, she would get there by herself. She worked hard and put her savings towards tickets for a rail journey across Siberia. It was 1932 when she reached Yangcheng in Shanxi province. There, for a while, she worked as a foot inspector for the Chinese Nationalist Government.[1] Meanwhile, she told those with whom she worked of the love of God.

In 1936, Gladys became a Chinese citizen and took in orphan children. Some of these she adopted as members of her own family.

Two years later, the Japanese started to bomb cities across China. Then they sent in troops, taking the lives of thousands of men, women and children and leaving large numbers of orphans. When Yangcheng was attacked, Gladys knew her family in England would be concerned for her, so she sent a letter home, saying,

> Do not wish me out of this or in any way seek to get me out, for I will not be got out while this trial is on. These

> are my people; God has given them to me, and I will live or die with them for Him and His Glory.[2]

Soon word came through that the Japanese were close by and approaching the city. The lives of both adults and children were in danger. The safest place for the orphans in her care was in the mountains nearby. From there, Gladys hoped to go down to the Yellow River and cross it to safety in Sian. The local mandarin provided baskets of millet and two coolies to help carry the load. They had four long, difficult, tiring weeks ahead of them.

She planned to take with her almost 100 orphans. About 20 of these were older girls and seven were older boys, up to 15 years of age. The rest of them were between four and eight—wild, shouting, laughing, crying kids, who climbed the rocks on the sides of the trail. Gladys used a whistle to bring them to safety and to call the roll to make sure none was missing.

As they pressed on, she could see that some of the older girls, whose feet had earlier been bound, were suffering from walking the mountain paths. However, like their leader and guardian, they made no complaint. Gladys kept anxious watch by day and worked to keep them safe as they slept. One night, an elderly Buddhist priest gave them shelter in his temple and, at times, they slept as well as they could in the open.

Soon the coolies who had been carrying the millet had to return to their village. After the food ran out, they came upon a band of Nationalist soldiers who fed them for one night. Then they had to go on without food and there was only a little water.

At last, they reached the river to find there were no boats available. They were in a war zone, with nothing to eat and with a mile of water between them and safety. With the young children calling for food, Gladys sent the older boys to scavenge in a deserted village. They returned with enough scraps for the younger ones, who ate as Gladys and the older ones looked on.

On the fourth day, there was still no sight of a boat to carry them across the wide, swiftly flowing Yellow River. By then, Gladys was thin, hungry and unsteady on her feet. The children huddled as close as they could to their only source of comfort and hope. It was then that one of the older girls reminded Gladys of the way God had opened the Red Sea for Moses. She then asked why God did not do the same for them.

"I am not Moses," Gladys replied wearily.

"But God is always God," the teenager persisted. "You have told us so a hundred times. If He is God, He can open the river for us."

So together they knelt and prayed, and after that they all bravely sang one of the songs Gladys had taught them.

Nearby, the commanding officer of a cluster of Nationalist soldiers heard an unusual sound. It was not the buzz of a Japanese plane on patrol. Through his binoculars, he was astonished to see that it was a crowd of Chinese children gathered at the water's edge—and singing loudly.

After the introductions, he signalled across the river for a boat. Three trips later, they were all transferred to where they could find shelter, food and safety. Of all the children who started the journey, there were no losses—all were accounted for.

What a joy to be able to say in the last day, "Here am I, Lord, and the children given to me!" How long do you suggest we have responsibility for taking an interest in the welfare—spiritual and otherwise—of those who have been given to us in our classes?

---

1 By then, the practice of binding the feet of young girls to keep them small was prohibited. Inspectors were hired to enforce the prohibition.

2 Alan Burgess, *The Small Woman* (London: Pan Books Ltd, 1959), page 149.

Motivation: the hidden factor

"If we live by the Spirit, let us also be guided by the Spirit. Let us not become conceited, competing against one another, envying one another" (Galatians 5:25, 26).

When it comes to the work we give our students to do, two important questions may be asked. First, how well are they doing it? Then, what is prompting them to do it? That is, what is motivating them?

There are two kinds of motivation. It can be *intrinsic* to the assignment—which means the pupil finds the work interesting and rewarding in itself. Or it can be *extrinsic*—which means they are making the effort to do the work for reasons outside the assignment itself. This could be to avoid punishment or it could be to gain something they value.

I saw an illustration of extrinsic motivation some years ago while visiting an Adventist primary classroom in a country area. The teacher was in his 30s and there were around 20 pupils in the room. During a mathematics lesson, I noticed a chart on the wall that listed the children's names in two groups. At the head of each group was the name of an explorer who, many years before, had opened up that part of the country.

At recess, I spoke with the teacher and showed an interest in the chart on the wall. He was happy to talk about it. The class was divided into two "houses" which were given points for the classwork their members finished during a set time. They were being motivated by the thought of doing better than others in the classroom.

After hearing the teacher's explanation, I asked if it was necessary to use this type of extrinsic motivation to encourage effort in mathematics. He replied with a question of his own, "You don't think, do you, that children can be naturally interested in mathematics? I don't like it myself!"[1]

There are some important things to be noted here. Those intrinsically motivated in a subject, whether Bible, mathematics, poetry, biology or written expression, are most likely to come back to it gladly in later life and perhaps build it into their lifework. As well, the most effective teachers will themselves find excitement in the subjects they teach. Then they are ready to pass that enthusiasm on to those in their classes. Most importantly, as our text for today reminds us, the kind of motivation we use can have an influence on the development of the learner's character.

Games at school generally involve keeping score, and this allows for learning to lose generously ("Congratulations, you played well") and to win graciously ("Thanks, you did well, too"). This is different from having the same teams struggling against each other week after week, month after month and, in some instances, even year after year.

As far as doing business in a competitive world is concerned, I expect that most of us would prefer to have a tradesman or dealer working for us who is motivated to do an honest job regardless of whether or not there are competitors looking on. It has been well said:

> God's plan of life has a place for every human being. Each is to improve [their] talents to the utmost; and faithfulness in doing this, be the gifts few or many, entitles one to honour. In God's plan there is no place for selfish rivalry.[2]

Besides, those who live by the Spirit and have the fruits of the Spirit have no interest in "competing against one another, envying one another" (Galatians 5:26).

Life beyond school is full of competition. If we remove it entirely from school life, are we then failing to prepare our children and youth for what they will have to face later in life?

1 I believe this teacher was a fine upright man who had not thought about the results of using a competitive scheme in his classroom. It might have helped if he had been able to discover that the study of mathematics can be full of interest and a lot of fun—then he could have helped his pupils to enjoy it as well. In addition, he had not realised the benefits of encouraging young people to do a worthwhile project for its own intrinsic value rather than by way of selfish motivation.

2 Ellen G White, *Education* (Mountain View, CA: Pacific Press Publishing Association, 1903), page 226.

The square brown desk

"[U]nless you change and become like children, you will never enter the kingdom of heaven. Whoever becomes humble like this child is the greatest in the kingdom of heaven" (Matthew 18:3, 4).

A few decades ago, I was handed a piece of poetry while visiting a North American university. It was titled "About School"[1] and it told of a child who could not find anyone to listen to what he wanted to say. So he found another way:

He would lie out on the grass and look up in the sky.
And it would be only him and the sky and things inside him that needed saying.
And it was after that he drew the picture.
It was a beautiful picture.
He kept it under his pillow and would let no-one see it.
And he would look at it every night and think about it
And when it was dark, and his eyes were closed, he could still see it.
And it was all of him.
And he loved it.
When he started school he brought it with him.
Not to show anyone, but just to have with him like a friend.
It was funny about school.
He sat in a square brown desk, like all the other square brown desks, and he thought it should be red.
And his room was a square brown room like all the other rooms.
It was tight and close, and stiff.

Sadly, school was a trial to him. Then came the class when they were free to draw:

And he drew all yellow and it was the way he felt about
morning.
And it was beautiful.
The teacher came and smiled at him.
"What's this?" she said.
"Why don't you draw something like Ken's drawing? Isn't
it beautiful?"
After that his mother bought him a tie.
And he always drew airplanes and rocket ships like
everyone else.
And he threw the old picture away.
And, when he lay alone looking at the sky,
It was big and blue and all of everything.
But he wasn't any more.
He was square inside.
And brown.
And his hands were stiff.
And he was like everyone else.
And the things inside him that needed saying didn't need
it any more.

To ensure that it might never happen that way in your class or mine, shall we think of these little ones as coming to us fresh from God's hands—and each one special in their own way? We may cooperate with the Spirit of God to encourage that specialness, rather than see it sadly discouraged.

Suppose we are looking at a piece of creative work by one of our students. Which might we better raise first: technical details (for example, punctuation and spelling in a piece of writing, or the order in which glazing is applied in pottery) or what the learner is trying to express of themselves? For this last option, what might we best say?

---

1 The full poem, written by an anonymous author, is readily available on the internet.

A word for sustaining the weary

"The Lord God has given me the tongue of a teacher, that I may know how to sustain the weary with a word" (Isaiah 50:4a).

During World War II (1939–1945), there was an interesting general leading the military forces of Britain. General Bernard "Monty" Montgomery (1887–1976) was a vegetarian and he did not smoke. He would not touch alcoholic drink and, wherever he went, he carried a small Bible with him.

In the early months of 1944, Hitler still had the continent of Europe in his cruel grip. But D-Day,[1] the commencement of liberation, was coming closer, and General Montgomery was to have a vital part in making it a success.

Such an important campaign needed a rehearsal. The leading British army officers, including General Montgomery, were on the beach in the south of England. The ships were waiting out at sea, war planes were flying overhead, and the landing craft were standing off the beach with the soldiers cooped up for hours, waiting to come ashore. Some of them were seasick.

At last, the order was given for the men to be landed on the beach and to march past the official party. At the worst possible moment, a teenage soldier, suffering terribly from seasickness and carrying a large pack on his back, tripped in his heavy boots and fell on his face in the sand. Sobbing quietly, he picked himself up in a daze and set off the wrong way with his pack dangling from his back.

What would Monty, the strict disciplinarian, do? Quickly, he was by the boy's side and speaking encouragingly: "This way, sonny. You're doing well—very well. But don't lose touch with the chap in front of you." Then he lifted the pack back into position on the boy's shoulders. The lad recognised the one who had helped him and he looked at Monty with "dumb adoration."[2]

Monty has gone down in history for combining discipline with kindly encouragement. For this, says William Barclay, "a private in [Monty's] Eighth Army felt himself as good as a colonel in any other army."[3]

Our children and young people will sometimes let themselves and us down. What shall we say when that happens? We could use ridicule and crush them. We could instil shame and self-doubt and give them heavy baggage to carry into adulthood. Or we could give them a bright and hopeful picture of themselves—a picture they can carry for the rest of their lives.

Isaiah spoke of teachers with a special gift—a gift for lifting up "the weary with a word." These teachers can recognise when their students are struggling to do well and are tired and distracted with burdens. Some of these burdens may come from home, in relating to parents and siblings. Some may come from trying (and failing) to fit in with others at school. Some may be about difficult subject matter in class. Because of these burdens, some of our students may fail over and over again. But when a teacher is calm, compassionate and gentle with a struggling student, perhaps even when a student needs something explained again and again, the student learns that they are important to their teacher and to God—that they have value.

Now that is not a burden to carry into later life! It is an assurance that can help to encourage any one of us through challenges.

And imagine how you would feel one day if one of your former students came to you and said, "It is because of you that I started to believe in myself and to set new goals for my life"?

As was said long ago: "If the only tool one has is a hammer, it's tempting to see every problem as a nail."[4] Gifted, loving teachers, of course, have other "tools" in their kit. Can we think of a few tools for encouraging students who are burdened, failing or have made mistakes?

1 It seems that the "D" in D-Day doesn't stand for any particular word. It was simply a useful way of referring to the commencement of an invasion without naming the actual date. This was handy when the exact day had not yet been chosen or was not intended to be widely known. In the end, the D-Day for the invasion of Europe was June 6, 1944, and that has become the most famous D-Day in history.
2 The full story is told in Clifton James, *I Was Monty's Double* (London: Rider and Company, 1954), pages 55, 56. James was there at the rehearsal to learn all he could of the way Monty spoke and acted, so he could play his part well.
3 See commentary on Colossians 3:20, 21 in William Barclay, *Daily Study Bible* (Philadelphia: The Westminster Press, 1975) page 164.
4 This idea was popularised last century by both Abraham Maslow and Abraham Kaplan, though it may be much older.

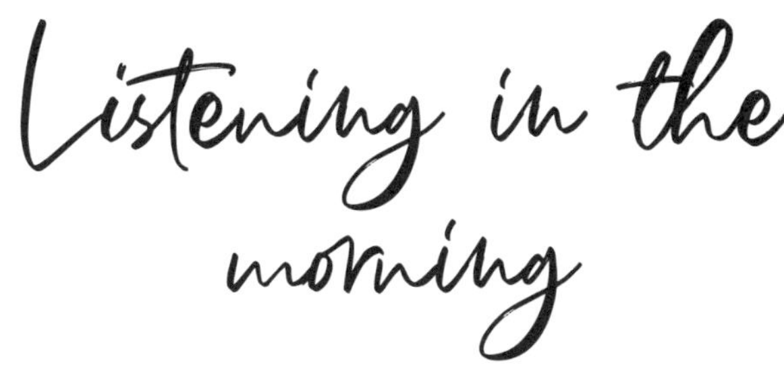

Listening in the morning

"Morning by morning he wakens—wakens my ear to listen as those who are taught" (Isaiah 50:4b).

William Murdoch was a young man living on a farm near the southwest corner of Scotland. There were 10 children in the family and each one had their appointed work—Willie cared for the dogs that were used to round up the sheep. He expected he would be a farmer all his life.[1]

Certainly, he had no interest in further study. His unhappy experiences in the village school had cured him of that. Then, in 1913, when Willie was 12 years old, something happened that changed things forever. A young Adventist colporteur called by, and Willie's parents invited him to stay with them while he visited the nearby farms.

Altogether, the colporteur stayed for three weeks and each evening, after the meal, the family would gather around the fireplace to study God's Word. Before long, the Murdoch family decided they would become Seventh-day Adventists.

Several years later, the principal of the Adventist college in the south of England travelled to the region to encourage young people to train in his school. Willie was not interested in going back to studying. Besides, the children were needed on the farm. And the Lord was coming very soon—there was no time to spend in training.

Before he left, the principal tried a new approach. He said to Willie's mother, "Sister Murdoch, you believe in tithing, don't you?"

She replied, "Yes, when we accepted this truth, there were no reservations. We sold our pigs. We stopped eating meat and drinking tea. We paid tithe and we kept the Sabbath."

"Did you ever wonder," he went on, "if God wants you to pay tithe on your 10 children and have one of them go to college and prepare to be an Adventist minister?"

She hadn't thought of that. She asked Willie, "Would you go to college?"

He did not need a lot of time to decide. "Certainly not! Excuse me!"

Others of the family went to college the next September. And more the following year. But still, Willie stayed on the farm. It was then that God stepped in.

Willie made an appointment with God and started to meet with Him up on the hillside. God knew that the young man was willing to "listen as those who are taught" and "wakened his ear" (Isaiah 50:4b). He asked Willie to forsake all and follow Him. Now he knew that he should go to school again—desks and books and study and all. The next September, he went to college and did very well.

Dr William Murdoch served in Adventist schools, colleges and universities for the rest of his working life. Of the 10 children in the Murdoch family, seven of them entered the work of the Seventh-day Adventist Church in various regions around the globe, including Africa, England, Australia, Canada, the United States and Tibet.

Waking in the morning is not so difficult. An alarm clock can do that for us. But *waking our ears* is something special. God did it for Willie and He can do it for us if we are ready "to listen as those who are [willing to be] taught." Then we too will know better how to fulfil our teaching ministry in the best possible way.

Have we experienced the difference that comes from listening for God to speak to us at the beginning of the day? What difference did it make? If not, are we willing to make time to listen?

---

1 The story was told by Dr W G C Murdoch in the Avondale chapel in 1953—his last year as principal of Avondale College (now Avondale University). The recording can be found in the University archives.

The flock as a priceless gift

"Lift up your eyes and see those who come from the north. Where is the flock that was given you, your beautiful flock?" (Jeremiah 13:20).

The king of Judah was in deep trouble. God had given him a heavy responsibility, and this he had failed to meet. It was not that he was too weak. It was not that he did not have the resources. Mostly, it was because he was too proud to admit he was going the wrong way. And now the day of reckoning had come.

It had to do with a flock—not a flock of sheep or goats, but a flock of living, breathing, hoping, choosing people. They were all looking for fulfilment and happiness. But were they looking in the right place? That was the question.

The king had not gone out and won this flock from one of Judah's neighbours. When he came to the throne, they were there waiting for him and were given to him by God. With the authority of kingship, he could point them away from the idolatry of all the nations around them. They needed knowledge and example and inspiration. And these he had failed to provide.

We too, as teaching evangelists, have been given a flock. They are all young and impressionable. Their parents have chosen us as guides to teach them what is best in life and what should be avoided. They are all looking for models to follow in finding fulfilment, success and happiness. They are waiting to see if we understand their hopes, their desires and the challenges they face. At the commencement of the school term, we found them there waiting for us.

Like the people of Judah long ago, they need knowledge of the results of certain types of behaviour. If they identify with us—as we hope they will—they will watch intently for our example. If they can catch a view of the One to whom we look day by day, they may be inspired to build their lives similarly.

Then, in the day of final accountability, when we are asked, "Where is the flock that was given you?" we may be able to respond, "Here am I and the children whom God has given me" (Hebrews 2:13).

With the end of His earthly work in view, Jesus prayed the great prayer we find in John 17. In verse after verse, Jesus spoke of those "that you have given me." In verse 14, He said, "I have given them your word." Some students may respond to God with baptism during the time they are with us. Others may do so later, and still others may never do so. We must leave the choice with each person. But whatever happens, let it be said that we have faithfully given them God's word.

Momentous new beginnings

"Let the little children come to me, and do not stop them; for it is to such as these that the kingdom of heaven belongs" (Matthew 19:14).

The boy Fufu grew up in a wealthy home and was badly spoilt. If the servants did not give him what he wanted, he would throw a tantrum, and he mostly had his way.[1]

At last, Fufu was sent to school—to a classroom with children eight or nine years of age. Again, he made a fuss if he did not get what he wanted, and it upset the class. Then, one of the teachers suggested he be sent to a lower grade to work with the youngest children in the school. They hoped it would improve the situation. In fact, something surprising happened.

One day, the children were in the lunch room for their midday meal. With his lunch pack open on his lap, Fufu found himself sitting next to a pretty and fragile little girl called Fufetta. She was wearing a flimsy dress with her thin arms and legs showing through. Glancing to his side, Fufu could see that the child beside him had nothing to eat. He could see, as well, that she was hungry and that she had heavy teardrops spilling down her lovely cheeks.

The young rebel had never before been in a position like this. He was gripped with shame at the thought of eating while someone else went hungry—and someone delicate and pretty at that. Hardly aware of what he was doing, he picked up his lunch and put it down on Fufetta's lap. Then, still not knowing what was happening within his troubled little soul, he stood, turned away and burst into tears.

It was then Fufetta's turn to take the lead. She stepped over to the side of the softly sobbing boy to comfort him—the way she would speak to her rag doll. She said in a pleading voice, "Do not cry, Fufu." Then she gently drew aside the arm that was hiding his face and kissed him.

At this, a further surge of feeling flooded Fufu's heart. He reached out with both arms and clasped the tiny girl about the neck. Then, through his tears, he kissed her in return. Soon, with a deep sigh, he dried his face. After that, he smiled as he'd never smiled before.

At that moment, a strident voice called from the end of the passageway: "Here, here, you two down there—be quick with you! Inside both of you!"

In telling the story, Italian writer Umberto Notari makes a sad comment. The one calling out so unfeelingly, he says, was "the guardian." She knew nothing of the "first gentle stirring in the soul of a rebel." And she crushed it with "the same blind brutality that she would have used if the two had been fighting." The keeping of the rule for everyone to go into class on time was apparently more important to her than encouraging a momentous new direction in a child's life.

But maybe that is an unfair judgment. Teachers, as well as children, have a host of burdens crowding in upon them. Maybe what she needed to understand was not just what her children were doing but why they were doing it. And that may require a good deal of sanctified imagination.

Instead of thoughtlessly crushing this golden moment in the soul of the rebel boy, what might the teacher have done instead?

---

1 The story is told by Umberto Notari in his book *My Millionaire Uncle* and re-told in Maria Montessori, *The Discovery of the Child*, translated by M J Costelloe (New York: Ballantine, 1967), pages 51, 52.

Coming with reverence

"Take care that you do not despise one of these little ones; for, I tell you, in heaven their angels continually see the face of my Father in heaven" (Matthew 18:10).

Notari's story of Fufu and Fufetta was introduced to teachers around the world by the Italian medical doctor, Maria Montessori (1870–1952). She wrote a number of books on the best ways to guide young children. She also opened her own schools and trained teachers to work according to her philosophy.

Montessori's classrooms had lots of things in them that children could handle to show they were mastering the tasks of growing up. There were frames for practising buttoning up, rods for arranging in steps, and weights for arranging in order. And there were lots of things to be matched—blocks with numerals, colours with colours, and geometrical shapes with the drawings of those shapes on cards.

Children had lots of freedom in moving about the room and going about their work. The teacher was to guide them and observe them with care. Montessori would often watch her teachers at work. On one occasion, a younger child in the room wanted to see what taller children in a group were looking at, so he carried a chair over, intending to stand on it. Realising what the child had in mind, the teacher took him under the arms and lifted him up. Montessori advised that in doing this, she had denied the child a sense of independence and achievement.[1]

She encouraged teachers working with children in the "sweet and tender age of childhood [to respect their development] with a kind of religious veneration"—rather like seeing "a flower just beginning to bloom."[2] In all of this, we may come with reverence as we join with God in this heaven-ordained work.

As already noted (see page 6), there are "developmental tasks" for each of the age groups, and our children and young people are intent on tackling these tasks from day to day to give themselves confidence that they are indeed growing up. It could be an interesting exercise for staff members to carry out some quiet observation of the way students are growing in these tasks and report back on this to a future staff meeting—without mentioning student names. This might lead to new strategies to support and encourage students. Ideas for kinds of behaviour to watch for can be found by searching the internet under the expression: "developmental tasks" and particular age groups.

---

1 This incident is taken from Maria Montessori, *The Discovery of the Child*, translated by M J Costelloe (New York: Ballantine, 1967), page 53. Much of the material referred to above is from this source.

2 ibid, page 50.

What shall we play?

"You know, in the schools of the world there is rivalry, and in the congregations of the wicked there is strife; their great ones are the victors in a contest, and their lowly members are despised. But so shall it not be with you" (paraphrase of Matthew 20:26).

The above paraphrase of Jesus' words to His disciples was written around the middle of the last century by a one-time Adventist teacher, Arthur Spalding (1877–1953). For a time, Spalding worked as secretary to Ellen White and also as a historian and writer of some important books. One of these is titled *Who Is the Greatest?* Despite its age, it is still a useful book for Adventist teachers who want to find the best kinds of motivation and incentives.[1]

The book makes its point with some memorable words: "Rivalry is a cancer that will eat the heart out of a Christian school and out of a Christian church."[2] In another place we are told: "Christian education is the remedy for selfishness; Christian education is the love of God in operation."[3]

It is clear that the upright leaders of tomorrow are in the homes and schools of today. Will the Adventist schools of today contribute to either of these groups for tomorrow? In the future, what will our present students do about the direction our society takes? What will they do towards guiding our church through the stormy days ahead? Will the future leaders be prompted by selfish ambition? Or will it be by loving service? To an extent, as church school teachers, it is in our hands.

Towards the end of the book, Spalding places rivalry in a wider context, especially the rivalry involved in competitive sports:

> The ball is in itself an innocent plaything, and might be used in co-operative play; but when rivalry, the spirit of

> war, seized upon it, it was made the field of strategy and stratagem, a training for war.[4]

The question of sports in Adventist schools and the playing of games with the keeping of score is not an easy one to answer. The above quote may be the closest Spalding comes to allowing that ball games may have a place in Christian education. However, even there he warns of a harmful spirit of rivalry.

Ellen White also treated the matter with care. She spoke approvingly of the way the teachers in Switzerland "enter[ed] into the sports of the children"[5] and called on teachers to "sometimes enter into the sports and plays of the little children and teach them how to play."[6] On the other hand, writing from her home in Cooranbong, Australia, at the time when American Adventist colleges were being established, she warned that their "sports and games [were opening] the door to a flood of temptation."[7]

In the education of our children and young people, where and by what means should the line be drawn in relation to rivalry? Much hangs on our answer.

What are the conditions under which team games are likely to be helpfully played in Adventist schools? How shall we judge whether these team games have been helpful or not? What can be said of sports days involving other Adventist schools or non-Adventist schools—are they less of a problem?

---

1 Arthur W Spalding, *Who Is the Greatest?* (Mountain View, CA: Pacific Press Publishing Association, 1941), page 32.

2 ibid, page 64.

3 ibid, page 57.

4 ibid, page 88.

5 Ellen G White, *Selected Messages*, Book 3 (Washington, DC: Review and Herald Publishing Association, 1980), page 228.

6 Ellen G White, *Testimonies for the Church*, Volume 6 (Mountain View: CA, Pacific Press Publishing Association, 1901), page 205.

7 Ellen G White, *Testimonies for the Church*, Volume 9 (Mountain View: CA, Pacific Press Publishing Association, 1904), page 65.

"To the one who conquers I will give a place with me on my throne, just as I myself conquered and sat down with my Father on his throne" (Revelation 3:21).

Westminster School has stood by the famous Westminster Abbey in London since the year 1179. Past students of the school include the hymnwriter Charles Wesley, architect Sir Christopher Wren and poet A A Milne, as well as seven prime ministers. One of the other students of Westminster School we know about not because he achieved something great but because of something daring he did in the Abbey next door.

Late on a summer's afternoon more than 200 years ago, this lad made his way into England's most famous church building. There he wandered around looking at the inscriptions on the tombs and up at the stained-glass windows. At last, he came back to the main doors and found them locked for the day. He was stuck inside!

Looking for a place to settle down for the night, his eyes soon fell on the famous Coronation Chair, the chair British monarchs have sat on to be crowned since the 14th century. And, sure enough, it was there that he fell asleep.

The story gets worse! Wakened the next day by the morning sun, he reached into his pocket—perhaps for something to chew on—and drew out a pocket knife. Having opened the blade, he turned around and coolly carved an inscription into the ancient oaken seat. It read: *P. Abbot slept in this chair, July 5, 1800*. And in that act he made more of an impression on the most famous seat in England than did the coming King George IV or any monarch who followed him.

What shall we make of the incident? Frank Boreham, who told the story, might have advised that it is best not to be read as a bedtime story to a growing boy.[1] And yet it reminds me of the high value God places on those made but "a little lower than the angels" (Psalm 8:5, KJV). Though we might not dare to sit on the Coronation Chair, Jesus promises those who conquer a "place with me on my throne, just as I myself conquered and sat down with my Father on his throne" (Revelation 3:21).

We should place this promise in the here and now. God intends a place for each of our students on His throne—the ragged, the unresponsive and the disheartened, along with the poised, the neat and the well-spoken. And our acceptance of them and our encouragement of their perhaps struggling efforts might help to persuade them that they'd like to sit there with us.

Then there are those with whom we mix in the school staff room every day. In God's eyes, they are intended for eternal honours. Shall we value them that way today? They will sense it in the way we listen to them, enjoy their stories (and their jokes!), value their judgment, and remember what they have already told us.

Jesus tells us that if we conquer we will share His throne, but He also calls us to serve and submit ourselves to others. It is the worth that Jesus places on all those for whom He gave His life that leads us to love and be loved, to respect and be respected. In comparison to serving out of a desire for approval or sense of obligation, what difference does it make if we serve our students and fellow teachers out of the quiet dignity of knowing our—and others'—value to God?

---

1 F W Boreham, *Rubble and Roseleaves* (London: Epworth Press, 1923), page 216.

Giving up all

"None of you can become my disciple if you do not give up all your possessions" (Luke 14:33).

Our text for today may be among the most demanding in all of Scripture. We are to "give up" all we own before we can begin to be counted as one of Jesus' disciples. Could this mean taking all that we possess, selling it and passing the money to the needy? Even becoming beggars ourselves? Surely, we could do more good over a longer time if we were to manage the distribution from year to year and from month to month.

We know well the individuals mentioned in the parable of the Good Samaritan—a traveller, a bunch of robbers, two religious leaders, a foreigner, and an inn-keeper. It is not a large cast. However, in a way, most of humanity is represented there by way of their philosophies of life.[1] There is the robber philosophy: What's yours is mine—and I'll take it whenever I can. There is the priest/Levite philosophy: What's mine is mine—and I'll keep it as long as I like. Then there is the Good Samaritan philosophy: What's mine is yours—and you can have it whenever you need it. We would do well, I suggest, to decide which of these philosophies matches our own philosophy most closely.[2]

These philosophies and the challenge in our headline text bring to mind the story of a wealthy old man who walked up a mountain one day with his greatest treasure at his side. God had told him what to do with that treasure. When he reached the top, he took it and bound it onto an altar—giving it up—placing it in God's hands. Then God said, in effect, to Abraham, "You've given your treasure to Me and I accept it. Now I place it back into your hands to care for. Remember who owns it. You are to manage it and you must give an account."

So Abraham walked down the slopes of Mount Moriah together with his foremost treasure—his son Isaac. They were the same two people, but now Abraham had a new relationship with his son and with God. He is an example of what it means to be God's steward—an illustration of what it means to give up all our possessions.

Instead of living as if all that is in my house, garage and bank account is mine, I might choose to give up all my possessions and place them, as did Abraham, as a love gift on the altar. Then I continue in a new relationship with my possessions. The same things may be there in my house, garage and bank account, but I am to care for them, use them and distribute them as His steward.

When I provide food and shelter, education and recreation for my family, I am doing it for God's children. When I plan for my own further education and training, I am doing it because my gifts are from God and they are to be wisely used and improved for further service in His name. When I provide food and shelter and education for those in need (near and far away), I am doing it at God's bidding for those others of His family. And, in all of this, I am to give account for the way I manage His resources.

Many of us are in a special category—we know how to teach!—and that talent is part of our treasure. This too is to be given up and placed on the altar. We are to follow God's leading about where, when and how we teach.

And if it sometimes seems hard to "give up all" for God, remember that He gave up all for our sake on that same mountain Abraham and Isaac climbed (we know it also as Calvary). He was the "Good Samaritan" who gave what was His to give us life.

The apostle Paul had something important to say about our present subject: "If I give away all my possessions,... but do not have love, I gain nothing" (1 Corinthians 13:3). So, then, it is not only whether I "give up" my possessions, but whether it is from a motive of love.

---

1 I'm thinking here of a philosophy of life as that which is at the centre of all we do—the principle we live by, whether we put it into words or not.

2 These philosophies have been referred to by a number of writers. For example, <www.sermoncentral.com/sermon-illustrations/77438/three-philosophies-the-good-samaritan-by-rodelio-mallari>.

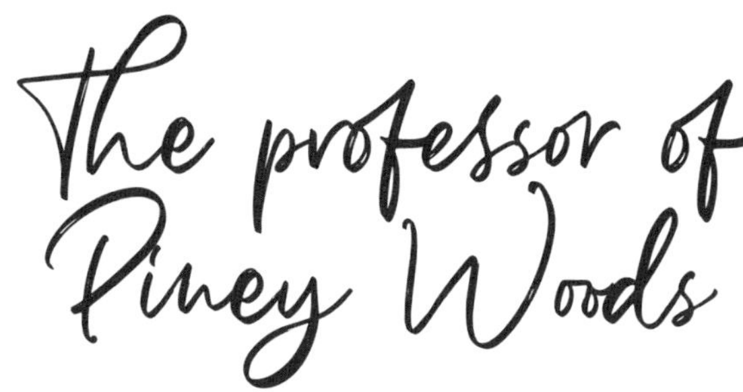

The professor of Piney Woods

"Only by such communion—the communion of mind with mind and heart with heart, of the human with the divine—can be communicated that vitalising energy which it is the work of true education to impart. It is only life that begets life" (Ellen White, *Education*, page 84).

Could you teach in a school that doesn't have walls or roof? A school without desks, a board or books? If they have to, schools can do without a number of things—but there are some things they must have for true teaching to take place.

James Garfield, a president of the United States, had no doubt regarding the most important feature of a true school. In 1856, while studying at Williams College in Massachusetts, he had a great teacher and said of him: "The ideal college is Mark Hopkins on one end of a log and a student on the other."

That has actually happened—not with Hopkins, but with another gifted teacher, an African-American called Laurence Jones. And it was the beginning of big things.[1]

Dr Jones graduated from the University of Iowa in 1908 and was wondering where he should do something worthwhile in teaching. In 1909, he heard that in Rankin County, Mississippi, 80 per cent of the population could not read or write. He accepted it as the call of God and took the train south.

Sad to say, this well-educated Northerner was not accepted with open arms. With a heavy heart and carrying some newspapers, Jones walked alone into the woods to think and pray about it. There he sat on a log, waiting for God's leading.

After a while, he noticed an African-American teenager watching shyly from the edge of the trees. Smiling, and looking the lad full in the face, Jones pointed to the log beside him and said gently, "Come and sit down."

As an act of friendliness, the would-be teacher passed the lad one of his newspapers. The youngster accepted it and held it fixedly in front of his face. After a few seconds, Jones looked across and noticed that the newcomer was holding the paper upside down. He asked quietly, "Are you going to read it?"

The reply was brief: "No, sir. I can't read."

Smiling, Jones looked into the boy's eyes and said, "Would you like to learn to read?"

Believing he could trust his new friend, the lad replied, "Oh, yes sir, 'Fessor, I surely would!"[2]

With quiet enthusiasm, Jones replied, "Then come back tomorrow and we'll make a start."

The next day, the boy was back—together with two others. By the time they had sung a hymn and finished their first Bible lesson, three more boys and seven men had arrived. Reading lessons followed. And Professor Laurence Jones's Piney Woods School was on its way.

By November, the class had grown to 50, so they rolled over some more logs and lit a fire out there in the open to beat the cold weather—that is, until one of the farmers gave them an old sheep shed that he wasn't using. They patched it up for a classroom. Donations of land and timber for a building followed. The people were being won over. This included the local African-American preacher, who gave Jones a heartfelt welcome before one of his sermons. He admitted that they had been doubtful of the young 'Fessor, and then went on to list some of his important qualities. Community acceptance was assured.

The curriculum was also taking shape. Along with Bible, reading, writing and arithmetic, they turned their minds to trades, farming, cooking and sewing. The students were to learn to think, to reach out to God, and to master three manual skills which could be used to earn a living.

Laurence Jones married three years later and his wife, Grace, supported the school through fundraising and the teaching of domestic science. It was an education built on developing the head, the heart and the hands.[3]

Jones was a man who knew the power of meeting his students face to face and mind to mind—whether one or many, on a log or at a desk. His story is a reminder of our opening reading. Here we are told that in true education there is imparted a "vitalising energy" and that ultimately this is between God and the student, as mind communes with mind and heart with heart.

As teachers, ours is the privilege of receiving a "double portion" of that energy from God and of sharing it with those in our classes.

It may feel safer to stand above our students. However, can mind truly meet with mind and heart with heart if we keep ourselves aloof? Are we ready to teach with our students at our side, with "the communion of mind with mind and heart with heart" leading on to the communion of the human with the divine?

Is there a nearby community that is waiting for a teacher to touch it in a new way with a "vitalising energy" so that "life begets life"—perhaps first of all with a branch Sabbath school or an adult literacy class?

---

1 The details given here are adapted from Beth Day, *The Little Professor of Piney Woods* (New York: Messner, 1955).

2 Teachers in America are sometimes called Professor. This shorter form, 'Fessor, is easier to say.

3 Laurence Jones led the Piney Woods School for more than 60 years, from 1909 to 1974. He died the following year, aged 92. The school is still operating near Jackson, Mississippi, offering grades 9 to 12.

A new pattern for the days ahead

"It was [God's] purpose that, as the human family increased in numbers, they should establish other homes and schools like the one He had given" (Ellen White, *Education*, page 22).

Early Adventist educator Arthur Spalding studied the origin of practices followed by popular schools of modern times. For example, he found that the origin of competitive games goes back to the ancient cultures of Sparta and Persia. There they believed their survival depended on military success, so the games the young men played were based on the skills needed in war. (It is not by accident that javelin throwing is part of the Olympic Games.[1]) In addition, Spalding saw the monastic institutions of medieval times as a leading model for modern schools.[2]

Spalding questioned if there was an alternative model set up by God for Christian schools. His answer was:

> There is. And this model is in many respects so different from the pattern of existing educational institutions that its acceptance and reproduction would constitute a major revolution. What is this model? The family, the home.[3]

Spalding went back to the Eden school for his authority. In the book *Education*, Ellen White wrote that this school "was to be a model for man throughout all aftertime."[4] It was God's purpose that,

> as the human family increased in numbers, they should establish other homes and schools like the one He had given. . . . Under changed conditions, true education is still conformed to the Creator's plan, the plan of the Eden school.[5]

The fact that there were no schools already patterned on the home did not daunt Spalding and perhaps it should not daunt us. There may be much gained in brainstorming those features of the home that might appear in a newly conceived classroom (and school) organised and conducted along these pioneering lines.

A basic core of ideas comes to mind, including intrinsic motivation, the incentive of love, the balancing of mental and physical effort, and the older and more advanced students encouraging the younger and less advanced. In consultation with the relevant authorities, a principal and any number of teachers (for example, as few as one or two) might work creatively in these directions.

If particular Adventist schools choose to move towards using the home as a pattern for their school, there are some important conditions that should be met. There would need to be enthusiasm and commitment from a number of directions, including education authorities, principals, staff, parents and students. Other conditions might include detailed planning of goals and outcomes, willingness to invest extended time in the project, and the laying down of comprehensive testing procedures to demonstrate that the new approaches have achieved their goals. Are there any others?

---

1 A W Spalding, *Who Is the Greatest?* (Mountain View, CA: Pacific Press Publishing Association, 1941), page 88.

2 A W Spalding, *Captains of the Host* (Washington, DC: Review and Herald Publishing Association, 1949), pages 434–438. See also page 645 for Spalding's comments on the influence of the ancient Greek philosophers.

3 ibid.

4 Ellen G White, *Education* (Mountain View, CA: Pacific Press Publishing Association, 1903), page 20.

5 ibid, pages 22, 30.

The glory-seekers

"I do not accept glory from human beings. But I know that you do not have the love of God in you. I have come in my Father's name, and you do not accept me; if another comes in his own name, you will accept him. *How can you believe when you accept glory from one another and do not seek the glory that comes from the one who alone is God?*" (John 5:41–44).

"[M]any, even of the authorities, believed in him. But because of the Pharisees they did not confess it, for fear that they would be put out of the synagogue; for *they loved human glory more than the glory that comes from God*" (John 12:42, 43).

People climb mountains for different reasons—perhaps for the exercise or the view or the sense of achievement. If it is a difficult mountain to climb, like Mount Everest, they might do it for the publicity and the glory.

On one of his visits to Mount Sinai, Moses had glory in mind—but it was a different kind of glory from that usually sought by humans. Speaking to God, he said: "Show me your glory, I pray" (Exodus 33:13). The Lord agreed and promised to make known His goodness as He proclaimed His name—and to experience that is to experience God's glory (see Exodus 33:19, 22).

Marvellously, it happened the following day. God proclaimed His name and linked it forever with His mercy, grace, patience, steadfast love, faithfulness and willingness to forgive all kinds of sin.[1] As a glory-seeker, Moses was wonderfully rewarded. He began to understand something of the glory that is at the core of the universe. It is not about sub-nuclear particles and the laws that control them. It is not a formula that relates mass, the speed of light and energy. It is what Jesus in His extremity on Calvary looked to—the heart of a loving heavenly Father. If only we and our children could catch something of *that* glory! Then we would feel no need to run after the selfish glory that is offered in this competition or that race, to be paraded as better than those around us.

The two texts given above from the Gospel of John are of special interest. It appears from John 5:41–44 that we can be glory-seekers in one direction only—from humankind or from God. If we settle on one, the other is put behind us. It is pointed out that we cannot be believers in Jesus and His way unless we choose to seek glory from God—that is, to understand how much He loves us. But since our hearts are by nature selfish, we will need to make the choice to go God's way anew each day.

Then, the second text tells us that where we choose to do our glory-seeking can be a test of our loyalty—whether or not we confess our belief in Jesus.

It may seem a small thing whether or not we offer incentives to our students to perform well. However, if we emphasise defeating others and being listed as first or top, the price turns out to be high. Our texts for today give us Jesus' summation of the situation—those who seek glory from humanity rather from God have placed themselves beyond believing in Jesus, the one who lived to serve in love.

So then, we have every reason to leave out glory-seeking from rivalry and competition and still more reasons to guide our students in improving the talents that God has given them.

Imagine the happiness, restfulness and enthusiasm of a class of students who have no interest in looking down on or defeating each other but instead see each other's virtues and want to encourage others and help them develop the gifts God has given them. I see them as among those who one day will hear God's "Well done!"

---

1 Interestingly, God added "yet by no means clearing the guilty . . . to the third and the fourth generation" (Exodus 34:6, 7). Perhaps this is meant to remind us that we live in a sowing–reaping universe. For example, if we choose an unhealthy diet, we will be forgiven; however, we will not be given back the teeth we have lost. Our children and grandchildren inherit the constitution we pass on to them. We know that "the wages of sin is death" (Romans 6:23). It is clear, as well, that sin often pays its wages promptly. It is not to be toyed with!

The first and worst sin

"For thus says the high and lofty one who inhabits eternity, whose name is Holy: I dwell in the high and holy place, and also with those who are contrite and humble in spirit, to revive the spirit of the humble, and to revive the heart of the contrite" (Isaiah 57:15).

"Do nothing from selfish ambition or conceit, but in humility regard others as better than yourselves" (Philippians 2:3).

There is a sin that got us into our present mess, and it might be the most common sin in all the world. It can be easy to pick it in others but much harder to see it in ourselves. In fact, it is hidden away in our hearts and minds where it can work without our knowing it. It prompts us to commit all kinds of wrongs towards others, from lying, cheating, coveting and stealing, to criticising and abusing others, even to murder.

It is called pride. It can also appear as conceit (having an exaggerated opinion of myself), selfishness (grasping as much as possible for myself), thinking of myself as above others and love of power over others.

Is being rich a sign of pride? What about being physically attractive, being good at academic studies or being capable at some art, craft or sport? C S Lewis thought otherwise:

> We say that people are proud of being rich, or clever, or good-looking, but they are not. They are proud of being richer, or cleverer, or better-looking than others. If everyone else became equally rich, or clever, or good-looking there would be nothing to be proud about. It is the comparison that makes you proud: the pleasure of being above the rest. Once the element of competition has gone, pride has gone.[1]

As teachers, this puts us in a special position. Perhaps, thoughtlessly, we have passed on to our students that their worth is somehow improved by their being better or faster or cleverer than others. We might even have made comparisons among those in the class. In doing this, we might have missed the chance to commend effort and improvement and might have made the pride problem worse for those in our care. Ellen White put it this way:

> At such a time as this, what is the trend of the education given? To what motive is appeal most often made?—To self-seeking. Much of the education given is a perversion of the name. . . . God's plan of life has a place for every human being. Each is to improve his talents to the utmost; and faithfulness in doing this, be the gifts few or many, entitles one to honour. In God's plan there is no place for selfish rivalry. . . . But how widely different is much of the education now given! From the child's earliest years it is an appeal to emulation and rivalry; it fosters selfishness, the root of all evil.[2]

Lewis saw similarly tragic character outcomes for those who are motivated by pride:

> As long as you are proud you cannot know God. A proud man is always looking down on things and people: and, of course, as long as you are looking down, you cannot see something that is above you.[3]

We need to keep in mind that humanity has been formed from the dust and returns to the dust (see Genesis 3:19; Ecclesiastes 3:20). As we are told in today's texts, we are to be contrite, with a sense of sorrow for our mistakes and for the selfishness of our hearts.[4] We are also to be humble, seeing others as better than ourselves.[5] But at the same time we are never to forget that we are made in God's image and that He values us enough to die for us. We are to be aware that we have been made but "a little lower than the angels" and "crowned . . . with glory and honour" (Psalms 8:5, KJV).

A wise Jewish rabbi put it this way:

> A man should carry two stones in his pocket. On one should be inscribed, "I am but dust and ashes." On the other, "For my sake was the world created." And he should use each stone as he needs it.[6]

Each day, we all have to face this first and worst sin in ourselves and others. It may prompt us to look down on our fellow staff members. It may tempt our students to be competitive towards each other. The cosmic conflict of the ages will be fought out in our own hearts and in the hearts of those in our care. Let mutual loving support be our watchword, the example of Jesus our inspiration, and the promptings of God's Spirit our guide.

Is it likely to encourage pride if we tell a child or young person that they are doing well? Will it do them harm to tell them that their work for the day is the best they have ever done? I believe not—so long as we do not spoil it by announcing that it is better than the work of someone else (or everyone else) in the room.

---

1 C S Lewis, *Mere Christianity* (London: Harper Collins, 2012), page 122.

2 Ellen G White, *Education* (Mountain View, CA: Pacific Press Publishing Association, 1903), pages 225, 226.

3 Lewis, *Mere Christianity*, page 124.

4 The Hebrew word for "contrite" in Isaiah 57:15 is *dakka*, meaning broken. Common English definitions are penitent, showing remorse and broken in spirit by a sense of sin. Most of us will be able to recall times when we have hurt others, when we have fallen short of the standard we know we should meet and when the sinfulness of our hearts has been made known to us by what we could be tempted to do should we take ourselves out of God's hands.

5 The Hebrew word for "humble" in Isaiah 57:15 is *shaphal* meaning low. Common English definitions are modest, lowly, not self-assertive, unpretentious, meek, the opposite of proud and having a low estimate of one's importance—but not presumably a low estimate of the importance of the gifts God has given us and of the work to which He has called us. A realisation of why we should be contrite (see above) should be reason enough for maintaining our humility.

6 Referred to in Philip Yancey, *Reaching for the Invisible God* (Grand Rapids, MI: Zondervan, 2000), page 93.

Miracle in Stony Valley

"The wilderness and the dry land shall be glad, the desert shall rejoice and blossom; like the crocus it shall blossom abundantly, and rejoice with joy and singing" (Isaiah 35:1, 2).

The city of Strasbourg lies in the far east of France, at the border of France and Germany. There, in the year 1740, John Oberlin was born. He was to have an important influence on the shaping of the school curriculum in several countries.[1]

Even as a child, John knew that God was close to him. He would pray the prayer that the high priest, Eli, gave to the boy, Samuel: "Speak, Lord, for thy servant heareth" (1 Samuel 3:9, KJV). At the age of 20, he wrote out a promise to God that included the words, "To Thee I consecrate my all!" And that is how he lived until his death on June 1, 1826, a few weeks before his 86th birthday.

John believed that God wanted him to be a minister, so he trained at a Bible college in Strasbourg. He worked first as a tutor for the children of a surgeon and then served as a chaplain in the French army. After that, at the age of 27, he was ready to commence his main life work as a pastor and teacher. His career lasted 59 years, and it was in the one place.

Fifty-nine kilometres (37 miles) south-west of Strasbourg is a location called Stony Valley. Conditions there were sad and sorry, with the people half-clothed and living in poverty. They spoke a strange mixture of French and German, which the people in the next valley could hardly understand. There were 80 families in all, struggling to stay alive on a diet mostly of wild apples and tiny potatoes scavenged from the depleted soil. Much of the land was littered with stones or covered by swamps.

John quickly understood that he would need to guide his people in care of the land and in raising a good variety of crops. When he was told the land in the valley would never grow anything worthwhile, he set about preparing the soil in his own garden and planting the kind of vegetables they all needed. His parishioners were amazed with the results and were now ready to follow his example.

They drained swamps and saved the manure from their cattle which they spread on their own plots of land. Then they planted flax, corn, grain and vegetables. John imported a better variety of potatoes and seed from as far away as Switzerland. He showed them how to graft stone-fruit and walnut trees and how to spin and weave wool.

The forward-looking pastor knew that as the community grew, they would need people skilled in a number of trades and professions. Capable young men were sent to Strasbourg to become carpenters, stonemasons, blacksmiths, glaziers and wheelwrights. A young man was sent away to become a medical assistant and several women to be trained in midwifery.

The schools in the valley were transformed. The curriculum included Scripture, history, agriculture and crafts, including spinning, knitting and weaving. A new standard was set in speech, with the earlier mixture of French and German replaced with standard French so that the people could interact with the world beyond the valley. This allowed industries and exports to spring up.

The vision and diligence of John Oberlin were abundantly rewarded. On his arrival, he found several hundred starving peasants, but after 50 years there were several thousand happy and prosperous farmers. John's new plan of education based on agriculture, crafts and trades quickly became known—first across France, then in Europe, and finally around the world.

Oberlin died in 1826, which was the year before Ellen White was born. It is evident that the approach he encouraged so successfully was well known to her[2] and she expanded it further. In her view, every student should be introduced to several trades and become "proficient in at least one."[3] "Brain and muscle [were to be] taxed proportionately"[4] and this she saw as improving readiness for the study of God's Word. Agriculture was given special mention. The student was to learn that "the hoe and the shovel, the rake and the harrow, are all implements of honourable and profitable industry."[5] As well, she encouraged the taking of physical exercise for those whose professions involved much sitting down and mental effort.[6]

In France, in Oberlin's day (for example, in 1750), 61 per cent of the population worked in agriculture. By 2000, this had fallen to 4 per cent. In England, in 1800, 32 per cent of the population worked in agriculture and this had fallen to 1 per cent by 2012.[7] *Does this suggest that the example of Oberlin and the counsel of Ellen White regarding the teaching of agriculture and trades is no longer important for Adventist schools in industrialised countries? What advantages might they still offer to students? What about in the developing world where up to 80 per cent of the workforce are still engaged in agriculture?*

---

1 The major source for this introduction to the life and work of John Oberlin is Gotthilf Heinrich von Schubert, *Memoirs of Felix Neff, John F. Oberlin, and Bernhard Overberg*, translated by Mrs Sydney Williams (London: Society for the Promotion of Popular Instruction, 1840), pages 39–57. The present writer had opportunity to visit Stony Valley on April 1, 1991, as the guest of the Adventist pastor stationed at Strasbourg.

2 This does not necessarily mean that Ellen White knew of John Oberlin himself.

3 Ellen G White, *Education* (Mountain View, CA: Pacific Press Publishing Association, 1903), page 218.

4 Ellen White, *Testimonies for the Church*, Volume 6 (Mountain View: CA, Pacific Press Publishing Association, 1901), page 180.

5 ibid, page 192.

6 Ellen G White, *Christian Education* (Battle Creek, MI: International Tract Society), page 183.

7 See <https://ourworldindata.org/employment-in-agriculture>.

"In all your ways acknowledge him, and he will make straight your paths" (Proverbs 3:6).

"If [the students in our colleges and training schools] have a living connection with heaven they will have an influence for good on those with whom they come in contact" (Ellen White, *Counsels to Parents, Teachers and Students*, page 549).

"You will know them by their fruits. Are grapes gathered from thorns, or figs from thistles?" (Matthew 7:16).

For most of his life, Jack Radley (1894–1968) worked for Adventist missions in the South Pacific. As a young man, he went with pioneer Adventist missionary Captain G F Jones on the maiden voyage of the *Melanesia*, departing Sydney Harbour on July 2, 1917. By the time of his retirement from his work as ship's captain, navigator and top-class engineer in 1955, Captain Radley had played a vital part in establishing the work of the church from island to island over a large expanse of the Pacific Ocean.

Captain Radley also served in the Australian army in Papua New Guinea for two and a half years (August 1943 to March 1946), assisting with translation, liaison with the national population and intelligence work.[1] In the early months of the war, he was approached by an American army captain and asked if he was a Seventh-day Adventist.[2] Upon replying that he was, he was told a fascinating story.

The army captain explained to Radley that his company of soldiers had been positioned inland at the north-east corner of New Guinea when a force of Imperial Japanese soldiers landed on the nearby coast at Buna. It was important that the size and exact location of the enemy force be known before they were resisted, so this captain was sent with 12 soldiers to survey the situation and bring back a report. They took with them a young New Guinean national.

The group managed to reach the coast and discover what they needed to know. Meanwhile, however, further enemy troops had arrived and the small group of allied soldiers found themselves hemmed in and unable to return inland to their company. Whichever path they tried, they could not get through. They realised they had just two options: try to fight their way through or to surrender. Either way, they expected they would all die.

The young New Guinean man who had come with them listened to the men talking it over. And then quietly he spoke to the captain and asked, "Why don't we pray and ask God to show us the way out? He will do it."

"But," the captain replied, "I don't know how to pray; I have never prayed."

"All right," said the young man, "I will pray and ask God to show us the way."

Then he looked in turn at each of those American soldiers who knew that their lives could be cut short soon and said, "Please take off your hats and kneel with me now."

So they knelt in a circle and the young man prayed simply from his heart: "Our Father, we need you. Please send an angel to protect us and guide us to safety. In Jesus' name, Amen."

Then he stood to his feet and said, "Captain, you and the soldiers, follow me."

The men replaced their hats, put their packs on their backs and followed the young man into the jungle. He walked without hesitation, sometimes turning to the left and sometimes to the right. To the wonder of the captain, there were no enemy troops barring their way at any stage. In good time, they all made it back safely, rejoining the main company of American soldiers.

With the group looking on, the captain said to the young national, "Where did you learn to pray and trust God?"

"You see," he said, "I went to a Seventh-day Adventist school, and there I learnt to trust God."

The captain told Jack Radley that he hugged the young man in appreciation and then fastened his watch on the young national's wrist "as a token of love for what he had done for [them]."

We do not know the name of the young New Guinean man or the Adventist school he attended. But we do know that, in this story, both he and his school passed the "fruits test" (see Matthew 7:16). What do you suggest it is about an Adventist school or college that encourages the type of trust shown by the young man in our story?

---

1 The war in Papua New Guinea extended from January 23, 1942, with the Imperial Japanese airforce attack on Rabaul, to August 15, 1945.

2 The present reading is adapted from a story written by Jack Radley and appearing in Rose-Marie Radley, *Captain Jack Radley and the Heyday of the Fleet* (Warburton, Vic.: Signs Publishing Company, 2018), pages 215, 216.

"The hands of Zerubbabel have laid the foundation of this house…who hath despised the day of small things?" (Zechariah 4:9, 10, KJV).

Some things start big and become small—like a snowman when the sun comes out or an ice cream cone in the hand of a five-year-old. Other things start small and grow much bigger—and I'm not only talking about acorns and holes in your socks. Here is how the largest Protestant school system in the world commenced in a small way in the hands of a man of faith, vision and courage.

In 1851, Goodloe Bell was a 19-year-old teacher living in Michigan in the United States. He worked hard and earned a reputation as one of the most successful teachers in the state. In 1866, one of his friends became ill and needed medical help. Just then, they heard of a new place that had opened that year in the nearby town of Battle Creek. It was called the Western Health Reform Institute. They discovered that it was run by the recently organised Seventh-day Adventist Church.

They went together to Battle Creek. Bell liked what he saw and took an interest in the teachings of the Adventists. After several months, he joined the church. Sadly, he worked too hard at his studies and, without sufficient physical exercise, his health broke down. So, in 1867, he went back to the Health Reform Institute. There, he worked in the garden and at other outdoor tasks.

At that time, an 18-year-old by the name of Edson White was doing summer vacation work in the type-room of the nearby Review and Herald publishing house. In his rambles between work and home, Edson came upon Bell sawing firewood behind the publishing house. They greeted each other and began to converse from day to day. The young man learnt that Bell was a teacher. This prompted Edson to tell Bell how much he disliked grammar, one of the main school studies of those days.

"But," replied Bell, "if grammar is taught well, it can be one of the most interesting studies in the world."[1]

"Would you teach a few of us?" asked Edson.

"Yes. Come around some time," was the reply.

Several days later, Bell answered a knock on his door and, to his surprise, found Edson White with more than a dozen young men standing there. Things moved quickly from there, with evening classes set up for young employees of the publishing house. One of them was John Harvey Kellogg.

Bigger things were soon under way. The members of the class were enthusiastic about the teaching skills of their young teacher. Edson's parents, James and Ellen White, looked on favourably. And Bell, in an act of faith, decided to resign his public-school teaching position, to move to Battle Creek with his family, and to set up a day school there.

At first, Bell had to rely on the fees paid by the parents of his students for his wages. Then the Battle Creek church paid him a salary to continue his day school teaching. He was the first Adventist school teacher to be salaried not by one or two families but by an Adventist church. The records suggest this took place in the early months of 1868.[2]

Then an important change took place. The General Conference of The Seventh-day Adventist Church decided that responsibility for Bell's School, providing a separate building in Battle Creek. The classes were to be held on the lower storey and he and his family were to live upstairs. The school opened on June 3, 1872. This has come to be seen as the first official Seventh-day Adventist school.[3]

From this small beginning, the church school system grew rapidly. By 1874, the church was ready to move into training its young people as church workers.[4] Movement was slow for a time, but things were to expand rapidly after the turn of the century. As noted in the Introduction, at the close of 2019 there were 9,489 Adventist schools worldwide, with a student enrolment of 2,044,709, making the Seventh-day Adventist education system the largest Protestant school system in the world.[5]

Who then could despise "the day of small things"? Shall we pray for wisdom to apply our foundation principles in the present day of opportunity and challenge?

As many non-Adventist and non-Christian parents choose Adventist schools for their children, in some countries children from Adventist homes may be outnumbered up to 8:1. What safeguards and checks might be put in place to ensure that the objectives of Adventist education are not pushed out of sight?

---

1 The story is told in Allan Lindsay, *Goodloe Harper Bell*, PhD Thesis, Andrews University, 1982, page 55.

2 Some short-term schools had been set up in earlier times by Adventist families. One of these was conducted in the early 1850s in New York State by Martha Byington with the encouragement of John Byington, later to become the first president of the General Conference. See A W Spalding, *Captains of the Host* (Washington, DC: Review and Herald Publishing Association, 1949), page 441.

3 ibid, page 443.

4 ibid, page 444.

5 <https://www.adventist.education/education-statistics>.

Christian education from top to bottom

"This is the work to be done in America, in Australia, in Europe, and wherever companies are brought into the truth. . . . Schools are needed where Bible instruction may be given to the children. The schoolroom is needed as much as the church building" (Ellen White, *Testimonies for the Church*, Volume 6, page 109).

As we saw in the previous reading, Goodloe Bell was conducting school in Battle Creek by around 1868, and by June 3, 1872, he was teaching in the first official Adventist school. However, at that time, there was no thought that schools like his should be replicated in Adventist communities worldwide. In her first counsel on education in 1872, Ellen White gave a broad view of the principles of "proper education," with important attention to the home. At that time, she was particularly focused on education gospel workers:

> We need a school where those who are just entering the ministry may be taught at least the common branches of education and where they may also learn more perfectly the truths of God's word for this time. . . . Those who really have good abilities such as God will accept to labour in His vineyard would be very much benefited by only a few months' instruction at such a school.[1]

Battle Creek College was opened for this purpose in 1874. In the 1880s and 1890s, six other worker-training colleges were opened across the United States, as well as one in Australia and one in South Africa. For 25 years, the church continued to concentrate on building its "educational structure at the top."[2]

However, there was a change on the way—and it came from an interesting direction. Ellen White arrived in Australia in December, 1891, and stayed until August, 1900. She spent much of that time working to set up and guide The Avondale School at Cooranbong, New South Wales.[3] Over the year-end of 1898–99, she attended an Adventist camp meeting at Hamilton, a suburb of Newcastle, quite close to Cooranbong. She was one of the speakers.

At this camp, meetings were held each day for the children of the campers and of interested people living nearby. We know a good deal of what happened in those meetings as one of the leaders of the group left a detailed description of what took place.[4] They helped bring about an important new expansion in Adventist education.

We are not told that Ellen White actually saw this work at first hand; however, it is captivating to think of God's servant making her way to the children's tent and watching the leaders tell stories from the Bible as the children listened with interest. She was impressed concerning what should be done and wrote about it soon after: "The good seed sown in these meetings should not be left to perish for want of care."[5] She counselled that:

> Workers in new territory should not feel free to leave their field of labour till the needed facilities have been provided for the churches under their care. Not only should a humble house of worship be erected, but all necessary arrangements should be made for the permanent establishment of the church school.[6]

And she had the whole world in view: "This is the work to be done in America, in Australia, in Europe, and wherever companies are brought into the truth. . . . The schoolroom is needed as much as the church building."[7]

This fresh counsel, together with the work being modelled at the Avondale School, prompted Arthur Spalding to note from America that "Australasia was to become for a time the leader in educational reform and expansion."[8]

Until then, Adventist schools had been mainly set up in larger church centres. Afterwards, in country after country, they began to spread out into provincial and rural areas. Secondary schools and academies followed.

In Adventist mission areas around the world, elementary/primary schools were set up in the opening phase of the church's work in new areas. Later, especially after World War II, secondary schools were needed in these same mission lands.

We are the heirs to these achievements from the past.

In view of the missionary heritage passed down to us, if a newcomer were to walk through our school today, what might they see that is distinctive of the Adventist church school system?

---

1 Ellen White, *Testimonies for the Church*, Volume 3 (Mountain View: CA, Pacific Press Publishing Association, 1872), page 160.

2 See A W Spalding, *Captains of the Host* (Washington, DC: Review and Herald Publishing Association, 1949), page 452.

3 The name "Avondale College" was not adopted until 1964. The original name was the "Avondale School for Christian Workers," then until 1964 it was called the "Australasian Missionary College." In 2021, it became "Avondale University."

4 See Ellen White, *Testimonies for the Church*, Volume 6 (Mountain View: CA, Pacific Press Publishing Association, 1901), pages 106, 107.

5 ibid, page 107.

6 ibid.

7 ibid.

8 A W Spalding, *Captains of the Host*, pages 646, 647.

Stairway through the stars

"How awesome is this place! This is none other than the house of God, and this is the gate of heaven" (Genesis 28:17).

He was a man from a godly home, single and leaving his family for the first time. Night came upon him and since there was no accommodation in sight, he had to sleep under the starry sky. Worst of all, he had a guilty conscience. He might have feared he had been forsaken by God. Perhaps there were no prayers that night.

Besides, look where he was! It was deserted and lonely and far from where his grandfather and father had conducted morning and evening worship through the years, far from where he had so often joined the family in prayer. Surely, it was no use expecting God to know anything of him in this lonely place. He threw his cloak over a stone and fell into a troubled sleep.

But wait! What was this? A stairway had been set up beside his stony pillow. It reached up through the canopy of stars and touched the doorstep of the throne-room of God!

As Jacob watched, he saw angel messengers place their feet on the top step of the stairway and make their way down. Others were making their way up. Then the greatest wonder of all—God Himself spoke, "I am the Lord, the God of Abraham your father and the God of Isaac.... Know that I am with you and will keep you wherever you go" (Genesis 28:13, 15). Jacob knew that the words were spoken to him, for God had mentioned his own grandfather and father by name.

It is no wonder that when Jacob awoke he was filled with awe and declared that place to be "the house of God, and... the gate of heaven" (Genesis 28:17). With the day breaking around him, he declared, "the Lord shall be my God" (Genesis 28:21). Not just his grandfather's God or his father's God, but *his* God.

This story is a reminder of some important realities. It is one thing to be a member of God's family around the parental altar but quite another to make a commitment to Him once we're facing life alone. In addition, some of us may be feeling lonely in our work—whether we're working in a one-teacher school or a staff school. If that is the case, remember that your classroom can be a house of God and a gateway to heaven. The stairway with the angels ascending and descending may rest beside your desk and mine. Each day, we too may hear God say, "Know that I am with you and will keep you wherever you go."

With the assurance that our classrooms have become a house of God and a gateway to heaven, shall we pray that our young people will be wonderfully aware of God's presence and that their learning may take place with a sense of security and confidence?

"Father, are you there?"

"Judas (not Iscariot) said to him, 'Lord, how is it that you will reveal yourself to us, and not to the world?' Jesus answered him, 'Those who love me will keep my word, and my Father will love them, and we will come to them and make our home with them'" (John 14:22, 23).

Blessed are they who can look back on at least one spiritual mentor—someone who by word and example has pointed them to a way of living close to God. While still in my 20s, I had such a one. His name was William John Gilson and for some years, he was the director of Adventist education in the southern states of Australia. We affectionately called him "WJ."

As WJ's assistant, I often travelled with him and heard him preach on many occasions. He loved the above text and I saw him as a living illustration of the closing line. WJ would sometimes read the following piece of poetry with meaning and it touched my heart. (The poet wants us to picture a child speaking.)

Are you there?[1]

I like to play close by my father's den,
Where he's at work, and every now and then
Ask: "Father, are you there?" He answers back:
"Yes, son." That time I broke my railroad track
All into bits, he stopped his work and came
And wiped my tears, and said, "Boy, boy! Be game!"
And then he showed me how to fix it right,
And I took both my arms and hugged him tight.
Once when I asked him if he still was there,
He called me in and rumpled up my hair,
And said: "How much alike are you and I!
When I feel just as boys feel when they cry,

I call to our Big Father, to make sure
That He is there, my childish dread to cure.
And always, just as I to you, 'Yes, son,'
Our Father calls, and all my fret is done!"

Most of us can tell if we are not as close to God as we may have been in the past. It was that way with a Papua New Guinean church worker who was attending a gathering of Adventists from a number of countries. He was asked to put on the heathen garb of his forebears so that the people could see the contrast with his present life. He replied, "When I put this on, the Spirit of God leaves me."

Let us not wait until our hearts are desolate. Instead, we can go alone to some quiet place and say, "Father, are you there?"

At what times are we likely to feel closest to God? Under what circumstances are we likely to feel distant from Him?

---

1 Strickland Gallilan, "Are you there?" in A L Alexander, *Poems That Touch the Heart* (New York: Garden City Publishing, 1941).

Ambassador in chains

"Pray also for me, so that when I speak, a message may be given to me to make known with boldness the mystery of the gospel, for which I am an ambassador in chains" (Ephesians 6:19, 20).

John Wesley (1703–1791) had a love for souls that would take him out of his bed in time to preach to the miners gathering before sunrise at the pit top. Then he would stay on to preach to those who had just finished their shift. As a true ambassador of the gospel of Jesus, this love prompted him to share a word of encouragement even with people he met for barely a minute, like the stablehand who took his horse when he arrived at an inn.

On one occasion, a highwayman bailed Wesley up on a lonely road as he was travelling to a preaching appointment. The masked man pointed a pistol at the evangelist and demanded his wallet. When Wesley handed it over, the highwayman swung his horse around and prepared to gallop away. However, Wesley had something else to give him. "Wait!" he called, and the bandit looked back. "Remember, the blood of Jesus cleanses from all sin!"[1]

Some weeks later, at the close of a meeting, one of the listeners pressed forward and placed a wallet into Wesley's hand. "I could not forget," he explained, "that if the blood of Jesus cleanses from all sin, it includes my sin as well."

True ambassadors—whether earthly or heavenly—keep in mind that at all times and in all places, they are to represent the government that appointed them.

The apostle Paul was such an ambassador. With God's authority, he told those within reach of his voice or his letters that God had already counted their sins against Jesus and that those sins were no longer being counted against them. He wrote, "we are ambassadors for Christ...we entreat you on behalf of Christ, be reconciled to God" (2 Corinthians 5:19, 20).

Flogging, stoning, shipwreck, hunger or nakedness could not stop this ambassador. Not even imprisonment in a Roman jail could stop Paul from speaking for Christ. It was there that this ambassador dictated the letter to the Ephesians, in which he asked for prayers. He prayed not to be given more comfortable prison quarters, not to be released, but that as "an ambassador in chains," he would be given the best words to relay the gospel message that had been entrusted to him.

How will it be with us? Will we take up the position of ambassador, representing God in the classroom, the church, the community and the education council? It has been well said: "If God has called us to be ambassadors for Him, let us not dwindle into kings or millionaires!"[2]

A parting word after even a short conversation may remain long in the thinking of one with whom we have been speaking. What prompts of this kind might we be able to use in the future? For example, "I believe we were meant to chat today" or "Call me if you'd like to talk some more" or "I'll send you something to read on this topic."

---

1 Wesley was quoting from 1 John 1:7.

2 This sentence is thought to have been penned by William Carey.

"Sir, we wish to see Jesus" (John 12:21).

For thousands of years, people have been composing stories. Many of these stories are fictional, but they show what the storytellers believed to be important to their communities. Around 400 BC, the ancient Greeks told a story like that. It was called "Gyges' Ring."[1]

Gyges, they said, was one of the shepherds of the king of Lydia.[2] He was a normal law-abiding citizen and did his work quietly and faithfully. One day, he was out in the fields when a storm burst upon him. This was followed by an earthquake, which opened up a cavern in the earth. To find shelter, he walked in and made his way down.

Soon, he came upon a large room, in which he found a bronze horse that was hollow inside with a door on the outside. Gyges went through the door and inside the horse he found a gold ring. He placed it on one of his fingers and made his way out.

At the next meeting of the king's shepherds, Gyges was wearing his new treasure. During the discussion, he happened to twist the ring on his finger so that the jewel faced inwards towards the palm of his hand. Just then, to his surprise, the others began to talk about him as if he were not there. Soon after, without thinking about it, he turned the jewel so that it faced outwards again. Then he found the others knew he was there. The story becomes tragic after that.

With such power in his hands, Gyges commenced a life of crime. He stole, he murdered and he released criminals from prison. Finally, he went into the palace where he persuaded the queen to join him, and together they killed the king. Then he took the throne.

Now we come to the point the ancient Greek storytellers had in mind. Could anyone with supernatural powers use them only for good—and not for selfish purposes? They decided it was not possible. But they went on to imagine what might happen if there were such a truly good man—a man who would not use his power to serve himself. This is what they decided: "The just man, then, as we have pictured him, will be scourged, tortured, and imprisoned, his eyes will be put out, and after enduring every humiliation he will be crucified."

Come forward now a little more than 400 years. Some Greeks have arrived at Jerusalem. I see them as carrying in their hearts the picture of the ideal just man. They hear of a teacher who calls himself the Son of Man. He is a worker of miracles and He doesn't use His powers for selfish ends. Some wait on His every word; others wait for an opportunity to take His life.

These visitors come upon a man with a Greek-sounding name: Philip—the name carried by the father of their most famous emperor. To him they put a request: "Sir, we wish to see Jesus" (John 12:21).

It was a moment of glory for heaven and earth—a few drops before a mighty shower, a handful of grain before a bountiful harvest. If these strangers could recognise the true Son of Man, so can all of those who carry a picture of the ideal in their hearts. When that One is "lifted up," they will be drawn to Him.

Shall we take time to pray that the imagination and hearts of our students will be captured for Jesus in morning worship, in Bible classes, in chapel, in weeks of prayer and through personal example?

---

1 The story has several forms. Perhaps the earliest was told by the Greek historian and storyteller Herodotus, who died around 430 BC. For this account, I've paraphrased and adapted the way the story is told in Plato's *Republic*, Part One, Book Two, written around 380 BC. Gyges name is pronounced "jigh-jeez."

2 Lydia was in the west of Asia Minor and its capital was Sardis, the location of one of the seven churches mentioned in the Book of Revelation. The area is part of present-day Turkey.

Seeking our "special place"

"Not more surely is the place prepared for us in the heavenly mansions than is the special place designated on earth where we are to work for God" (Ellen White, *Christ's Object Lessons*, page 327).

An Englishman came to serve in the South Pacific in the mid-1900s. He was a gifted administrator, preacher and storyteller. Here is one of the stories he told to a group of church school teachers and to me personally, when I spoke to him about it while visiting the United Kingdom. I believe it should not be lost to the present generation of Adventist church workers.

The central character is a young man we shall call Ernest. In the early 1900s, he arrived at the Adventist training college in England to prepare to be a pastor and an evangelist. Even while he was still in his teens, anyone could see that he was specially gifted as a public speaker. He looked the part. He had a good voice. And when he took worships in the dormitory or spoke in the chapel, he knew how to hold interest. Ernest also did well in his studies. He knew the teachings of the Seventh-day Adventist Church and how to defend them from the Bible.

Then came graduation, followed promptly by a church appointment. Still things went happily, with approval from his fellow workers and from those who heard him preach.

A major test came when he was asked to lead a mission team of his own. The hall was chosen. The advertising leaflets were printed and distributed and the people came. They liked what they saw and heard, so they came back week after week.

Then came a change. It happened after Ernest began to preach on "distinctive" Adventist subjects, like the Sabbath. He found himself talking to smaller and smaller audiences. This set him to thinking about himself and his future. He began to wonder if his gifts were meant to be used within the Seventh-day Adventist Church after all. Perhaps he should look for a larger church community in which to do his preaching—and that is what he did. He found employment with an alternative Protestant denomination and later with a still larger denomination.

My English friend had known Ernest from their childhood days and kept in touch with him from time to time. So it was that some decades later, he and his wife were back in England and they arranged to call on Ernest on a Sunday afternoon in autumn.

For quite a while, they spoke of mutual interests. Then the visitor glanced at his watch and said, "We must not keep you. It will soon be time for you to go down to the church for the evening service." At this, Ernest smiled faintly and replied, "There is no hurry. It is harvest time and the people stay out working in the fields. I shall go soon to the church. They like to think that their minister is there praying for them."

The passage at the head of this reading speaks of two things that are surely planned for each of us. One of these is a place in the heavenly mansions in which we are to live. (You will remember Jesus' promise in John 14.) The other is a particular place on earth where we are to work for God—and this second place is just as surely chosen for us as is the first. What a joy to believe that we have found that place—whether the audience or the classes are small or large!

Our young people may wish to adopt the spirit of the following poem in choosing their future work:[1]

> The happiest place on earth for me
> Is where my God would have me be;
> The happiest thing for me to do
> Is work my God has called me to.

What do you see as the central message of the above story? What do you suggest is not a safe guide for settling on the special place—or places—where we might best serve?

What principles might we follow in guiding our students in settling upon their future work? (Here are some suggestions: Pray for God's leading. Evaluate gifts and settle on interests. Seek counsel on particular occupations that match gifts and interests. Ask trusted friends for advice on further training and openings for service.)

---

1 The piece is quoted here from memory. The author is unknown.

"[T]he book of life of the Lamb slain from the foundation of the world" (Revelation 13:8, KJV).

Mount Stromboli is an active volcano, standing almost 1000 metres (3300 feet) high, off the north-east corner of the island of Sicily. At night, its eruptions can be seen from great distances so that it has been named "The Lighthouse of the Mediterranean." On one occasion, a minister was travelling by ocean liner in the Mediterranean Sea.[1] After darkness had fallen, he made his way to the ship's deck and stood at the railing. Just then, a brilliant column of fire burst from Stromboli's crater, lighting up the night sky and reflecting back from the canopy of dark clouds above.

As a writer of sermons, the preacher saw in the incident an apt illustration. He realised that the resplendent display from the volcano was intermittent—in fact, the first that he had seen. Then it came to him that at the source of the splendour—the fiery centre of the earth—things are like that all the time.

He compared the brilliant volcanic display to what took place at Calvary. It happened on just one day in history, but it gave witness to what the heart of God has been like from the beginning of time—and always will be like into eternity. Think for a moment of what the Cross teaches us.

First, it has much to say about sin. Sin is so bad that it took Jesus' death for the universe to be cleansed of it. The poet and preacher George Herbert (1593–1633), put it this way:

> Who would know Sin, let him repair
> Unto Mount Olivet; there shall he see
> A man so wrung with pains, that all His hair,
> His skin, His garments bloody be.

Sin is that press and vice, which forceth pain
To hunt his cruel food through ev'ry vein.

Second, the Cross tells us about justice. There is a deep mystery here—one that we may be meditating upon into eternity—so we must approach with reverence and humility. Truly, humans have violated the deep laws of the universe. But why not simply say, "Promise to do better next time and we will forget about it"? Is there something healing about punishment and retribution? If a just penalty is not exacted, will peace, goodness and true happiness be spoilt forever? What if the wrongdoer is too weak and helpless to bear the penalty? Is there some legal covenant that clears the way for a sacrificial substitute—even of the Lawgiver Himself?

The Bible gives some important clues in looking for answers to our questions. The first death on the planet occurred to provide clothing when our original parents chose to go against their Creator (see Genesis 3:21). In the sanctuary in the wilderness, the shedding of blood was central to making atonement (see Leviticus 16). Isaiah told of a "suffering servant" who was to be "wounded for our transgressions" and to have "laid on him the iniquity of us all" (Isaiah 53:5, 6). Then, in the "fullness of time," the "Lamb of God" came to take away the "sin of the world" (John 1:29). Since we are sinners, justice demands that we must die—and we have already done this through Jesus, for "one has died for all; therefore all have died" (2 Corinthians 5:14).

As well as telling us about the depths of sin and the need for justice, the Calvary drama is a declaration of love—"God's final refusal to let us go."[2] No matter what we do to our God and Saviour, there is nothing "in all creation" that "will be able to separate us from the love of God in Christ Jesus our Lord" (Romans 8:39).

These then are fiery elements forever in the heart of God—elements that existed from the foundation of the world and broke through in a cosmic tryst at Calvary:

Justice that will not let us off—love that will not let us go.

It has been suggested that it took no time to prepare a cross for Jesus' crucifixion. There was already one made up for Barabbas, who had just been released and would not need it now. I wonder what he might have said when he arrived home and whether he would have acknowledged that Jesus took the cross that was meant for him. The cross of Jesus still faces each generation of humankind. As we file over Golgotha, we may take up the hammer and drive the nails in further or we may bow our heads in worship, in thankfulness and in obedience. Regardless of how Barabbas responded, shall we respond in love and thank God for His sacrifice every day of our lives?

---

1 Believed to be Leslie Weatherhead.
2 The expression is from an E H Heppenstall sermon.

Jim's substitute

"But he was wounded for our transgressions, crushed for our iniquities; upon him was the punishment that made us whole, and by his bruises we are healed" (Isaiah 53:5).

A long time ago, there was a village in the hills that had never had a school. After a time, a school was started and children of all ages and sizes were sent along so they could learn to read and write and do arithmetic.[1]

I have to tell you that things started badly. There was bullying and cheating and swearing and a lot more things like that. Things were so bad that the first teacher decided to quit. Then another teacher, George Brown, applied for the job. The chairman of the school board warned him that it would be hard. He replied, "I will do my best."

On the first morning, George Brown faced his class. They were an odd lot. Some were so small that their feet didn't touch the floor when they were seated. Some were as tall and heavy as the teacher himself. Many were poorly dressed.

Mr Brown tried to be cheerful. "Good morning!" he said brightly. But the children just stared back, looking glum.

"We can have a good school, if we want to," he went on to say. Some of the class pulled faces and some laughed.

The new teacher continued, "A good school needs to have some rules that we all decide to keep. What rules would you like?"

They did not expect to be asked about rules. They thought about it for a minute and one of them called out, "No bullyin'!" The teacher wrote on the board, "No bullying."

Someone else called out, "No stealin'." The teacher wrote on the board, "No stealing."

"No lyin', neither," someone else called out, and this was written up on the board too.

The list went on until there were 10 rules written up. Then Mr Brown smiled and said, "You've done very well. If we follow these rules, we'll have a happy school." He paused for a few seconds, and then he went on, "For every set of rules there needs to be a penalty for breaking any of them. What should the penalty be?"

One of the older boys said, "The penalty should be 10 strokes across the back with a hickory stick."

Another boy added, "Coat off."

The teacher looked surprised and worried. "That is a harsh penalty. Are you sure it is what you want?"

They all nodded—from the smallest to the biggest of them. So he wrote under the rules, "Penalty for breaking one of these rules: 10 strokes across the back with a hickory stick—coat off."

Things went well day after day and week after week. Then came a sad and difficult day. Big Tom, the tallest boy in the school, came in at lunchtime and said to Mr Brown, "My lunch has gone. I think someone has taken it."

They looked at the board and saw the second rule: "No stealing."

They looked around and asked some questions and they found who had done it. It was Jim, the smallest boy in the school.

After lunch, Mr Brown called Jim to come to the front of the room. Slowly, he came forward, holding his coat collar tightly around his neck. "Please, sir," he said, "you can hit me with the hickory stick. But please . . . can I leave my coat on?"

The teacher swallowed hard and said, "The penalty says, 'Coat off,' Jim."

So, Jim let go of his coat and it fell to the floor. Everyone gasped. Jim's back was bare and his trousers were held up by a thin rope over each shoulder. They could see his ribs showing through the skin. He was a thin and hungry boy.

How can I beat him? thought Mr Brown. Then he remembered how bad and sad the school was before.

"Bend over, Jim," he said. And he raised the stick.

Suddenly, there was a call from the back of the room, "Sir, sir! Please, don't hit him. He's too weak and he's too small!"

It was Big Tom. He walked to the front of the room and threw his coat onto the floor. "Do it to me instead," he said.

The teacher put down his stick. Facing the class, he asked, "Our rules have helped to make this a happy class. The chosen penalty doesn't say who is to take the punishment. Shall we let Tom take the penalty in Jim's place—to be a substitute for him?" They all nodded their heads.

The stick came down 10 times. It hurt, but Tom didn't cry out.

Then everyone watched to see what Jim would do. He walked over to Tom and, reaching up, he put his arms around his big friend's neck and said, "I'm sorry, Tom, for taking your lunch. Thank you for taking my beating for me. I'll love you 'til I die." Then Tom hugged Jim, and they put on their coats and went back to their seats.

It was the same classroom as before, with the same people in it, but it was somehow different. Now the children kept the rules—but not because of the penalty. Now they loved each other and didn't want to bully, lie or steal. The worst school had become the happiest school and the best school. And the students took turns quietly sharing their lunches with those who were hungry.

Which would have been best for the happiness of the school—for the punishment to have been let pass for that time, for Jim to have taken his own punishment or for Tom to take it for him? Why?

---

1 This story is believed to have been first published in the early 1960s in an American Adventist journal for juniors. The present writer has been unable to locate the original. It is told here from memory.

Pray, listen, watch

"Before they call I will answer, while they are yet speaking I will hear" (Isaiah 65:24).

American preacher Phillips Brooks (1835–1893) is said to have been walking down a quiet street when he came upon a young boy in difficulty at the doorstep of a house. The lad was standing on tiptoe and struggling to reach the door knocker. Happy to be of help, Brooks lifted him up until his face was level with the knocker. A small hand reached out, took hold of the knocker and gave it three hearty bangs against the door.

Once on his feet again, the youngster looked up at his helper and said with a mischievous grin, "Now, let's scoot!" Then he scampered away around the corner.

Just then, the lady of the house opened the door and the embarrassed preacher was left trying to explain what had happened.

This led Brooks to wonder if we too sometimes play "knock and run" in our prayers. The Holy Spirit lifts us up to reach the knocker of heaven. We make our requests. Then we "scoot" without waiting to listen for any answer that God may have for us.

Maybe we should be watching as well as listening for heaven's answers to the petitions we make—as illustrated in the following true story.[1] Interestingly, it also features a front-door encounter.

The daughter of a Chicago millionaire was lame due to a chronically displaced hip and they knew of no surgeon who could help them.[2] At last, the family contacted Adolf Lorenz (1854–1946), an Austrian surgeon who had pioneered a procedure to correct hip displacement using "bloodless surgery"—realignment of bones through traction and casts. Dr Lorenz travelled to America at great expense to the family and took on the difficult case. After several months of treatment, Dr Lorenz's work proved a success—the little girl could walk normally! Word flashed around the world and he became famous overnight.

During his stay in the United States, Dr Lorenz was invited to make a tour of hospitals across the country to explain his techniques. As he travelled across the country, he received many requests for his help. Understandably, his schedule was so tight that the great majority of these had to be declined—and this makes an event in a mid-western city all the more poignant.

It happened like this. Late one afternoon, after a tiring day, the gifted doctor managed to slip past the bunch of minders assigned to protect him. Soon, he was out in the housing area and walking briskly. Without warning, a violent storm came up and threatened to soak him. Quickly, he stepped up to the nearest front door and rang urgently on the bell. The door was opened by a woman with an anguished face. She listened while the unexpected visitor, speaking with a foreign accent, requested shelter. Then she said, "There is trouble enough in this house. Go somewhere else!" After that, she shut the door and turned away.

Fortunately, the doctor did not have to stand long in the rain. His minders had set out by car to search for him, and they quickly pulled up beside him. He was soon back at his hotel with a change of clothing.

So much for Dr Lorenz. But what happened to the housewife who had refused to let him in? And what was the "trouble enough" in her house? She went to a bedroom where her daughter was lying in need of medical help. Earlier, she had heard that a surgeon from Europe could give the kind of help she needed and that he was coming to that very city. She had written a letter to the hotel where he was due to stay, pleading that her daughter might be able see him. But all she got was a bedraggled foreigner standing in the rain at her front door.

The following day the mother discovered what had happened. There on the front page of the local newspaper was a picture of the famous surgeon—and she realised she had turned down God's answer to her plea.

What are some ways that God might speak to us in answer to our prayers, if we will only wait, watch and listen? For example, have you had an answer to prayer through a passage of Scripture, the words of a hymn or a book, or something a fellow-teacher or friend has said?

---

1 The story is from Fulton Oursler, *Modern Parables* (Kingswood, Surrey: Cedar Book, 1955).

2 See <https://doi.org/10.1007/s00264-020-04620-y>.

Travelling light

"They confessed that they were strangers and foreigners on the earth, for people who speak in this way make it clear that they are seeking a homeland" (Hebrews 11:13, 14).

"Remember Lot's wife" (Luke 17:32).

Our denominational name, "Seventh-day Adventist," points back to Creation and points forward to the Second Coming. It reminds us that God was there at the beginning of earth's history and that He will be there at the end to welcome into an earth made new those who are committed to being His children.

Those of us who have taken that name are journeying towards the great climax of history. Is there some way to tell if we have loaded our travel bags in the best way for this most important journey? Here is a story that may give us some clues.[1]

The last shah of Iran held office from 1941 to 1979. He oppressed his own people, but he was friendly to foreign nations and gave security to foreign companies. During that time, an Englishman was working as manager of a business that supplied earthmoving equipment across Iran. Sales were high and so was his income.

The time came for the family to take home leave and return to England for several months. The manager's wife and their children left first. He arranged to follow them after he had completed some important company business.

It was in that waiting time that the Iranian Revolution came to a head. Supporters of the religious leader Ayatollah Khomeini drove the shah into exile and a new style of government was set up.[2] With little warning, there was a dramatic change to life in the city of Tehran. Contact with the rest of the world was cut off. The airport, with craters in the runway, was closed. There was no way for the manager to get in touch with his wife and children. He did not know where they were or how they were coping, and he knew they could know nothing of him. He was completely alone, and he did not know if he would ever see his family again.

However, he could not give up without a struggle. Every possible means of escape was followed up—by land, by sea and by air. Each was rejected as hopeless. Then one day he heard a rumour that the shell holes in the airport runway were being filled in. It was said that some of the embassies were planning evacuation flights for their remaining staff. Here was a glimmer of hope; but his inquiries showed that the waiting lists were impossibly long.

Then the phone rang. The caller would not give any identification. He had a short message and a brief set of instructions. In 30 minutes, the former manager was to be at the airport and he was to be wearing a plain white shirt and dark trousers. Importantly, he was to be carrying nothing more than a British Airways cabin bag. If he could be there in time, they would try to get him on board a British Airways flight disguised as a member of the crew.

His pulse quickened. Was it a way out at last or was it a cruel trick? Was it a looter trying to get free access to the house? What could he choose from all the possessions around him that would fit into one cabin bag?

With regard to the last query, the answer to just one question was all he needed to know: *What will help me to rejoin those I love most?* Silver cutlery and expensive wall hangings gave way to a few practical items for the journey—a toothbrush, socks, handkerchiefs. He had a single-minded focus on getting back to his family. He knew where he wanted to be. Iran was no longer his home. He was a "stranger and foreigner" set on returning to his true "homeland" (Hebrews 11:13, 14).

Within the specified 30 minutes, the door was closed on his former treasures and he was at the airport. Shortly after, he was winging his way towards London, freedom and the people he loved.

Lot's wife is one of the few characters of the Old Testament that Jesus referred to by name. He told us to remember her—to learn from her experience. Lot's wife had the opposite experience to our business manager in Iran. It was one thing for the angel to drag Lot's wife out of the city of Sodom. It was another thing to get Sodom and its luxuries out of her heart. The call to leave her old home for a new one came suddenly—while life was going on as usual—and her actions showed that her heart was in the doomed city.

Could it be that our challenge is not so much to get ourselves into heaven one day but to get heaven into our hearts now? And it is not a challenge but a joy if, like the manager, we keep focused on all that our true homeland holds for us.

Do we see ourselves as strangers and foreigners on the earth, as those who are "seeking a homeland"? Or are we like Lot's wife, clinging to a doomed city? The question is worth asking often—not of others but of ourselves.

---

1 The story is adapted from Robert Allaburton as told to Trevor Lloyd in "The cabin bag," *Adventist Professional*, 12(3), September, 1990, pages 29, 30.

2 The shah left Iran on January 17, 1979, and the Islamic republic was set up on 1 April.

The two shopkeepers

"The heart is deceitful above all things and beyond cure. Who can understand it? I the Lord search the heart and examine the mind" (Jeremiah 17:9,10, NIV).

"A new heart I will give you, and a new spirit I will put within you" (Ezekiel 36:26).

"[L]ove one another with mutual affection; outdo one another in showing honour" (Romans 12:10).

An old Jewish story tells of two shopkeepers living on opposite sides of a street in a busy shopping area. Day after day, they watched each other for fear that one might outdo the other. The matter came to a head when an angel visited one of the shopkeepers with an amazing offer.

"You may have," said the visitor, "anything that you wish—on just one condition. You must understand that the shopkeeper across the street will receive twice as much of whatever you receive. You have 24 hours to decide what you will ask for."

There followed a sleepless night and a stressful day. Again and again, the shopkeeper thought of something he longed for, only to have the thought turn sour as he anticipated a double amount of the longed-for thing being delivered across the way. Could he bear that?

Finally, as promised, the angel returned and asked if the shopkeeper had made up his mind.

"Yes," he replied. "I choose that I might . . . lose the sight of one eye."

This is not the first time we have looked at the effect of sin on human hearts. But this time, I want to focus on a remedy that can be applied to these "desperately wicked" hearts of ours. It was brought to my attention when I told this story in a sermon preached at a church in Sydney, Australia. After the closing hymn, three fresh-faced, bright-eyed young women came to me and announced that they had thought of a gift that the shopkeeper could have requested—and with a wonderful outcome.

When I smiled and nodded my encouragement, one of them explained, “He should have asked for the gift to be able to love his neighbour dearly. Then he would have been loved twice as much as that in return.”

These young ladies were English-speaking members of a church that held its services in a language other than English. (My sermon was translated.) I was impressed by their insights and would be pleased to learn they have become teachers, perhaps even back in the homeland of their parents.

Their proposal reminded me of God’s promise to Ezekiel. God wants to give His people the gift of a “new heart” and a “new spirit”—replacing envy, greed, bitterness and judgment with selfless, overflowing love.

Would it worry us if a co-worker had gifts and talents like ours but better? What difference would it make in our hearts or in the atmosphere of the workplace if we rejoiced at the gifts of others or additional opportunities offered to them?

John Pettigrew's mirror

"[Jesus] saw men as they might be, transfigured by His grace. . . . To many a despairing one there opened the possibility of a new life" (Ellen White, *Education*, page 80).

"[W]e have been buried with [Jesus] by baptism into death, so that, just as Christ was raised from the dead by the glory of the Father, so we too might walk in newness of life" (Romans 6:4).

As noted in another of our readings, some of the stories that communities share tell of things that didn't actually happen, but they are still important because they are about things the community values. This story is like that.[1]

John Pettigrew was an honest and hard-working basket-maker, living alone by the seashore in Cornwall, in the south-west corner of England. So close was he to the ocean that his yard was up against the sea wall. At high tide, he could hear the waves crashing against it.

John had only one relative in the village—a married cousin called Sarah Polgraine, who would come in to help with his cooking and cleaning. He appreciated her help even though she was forever grumbling and finding fault with her neighbours. When he spoke kindly of them, she would say, "The world would be a safer place if some old fools would learn to face the facts!"

One afternoon, after a summer storm, John took a sack and walked along the beach to pick up driftwood for his fire. Looking out beyond the breakers, he enjoyed the sight of a mother seal and a young one playing in the waves.

Just then, a flash of lightning and a roll of thunder warned him that it was about to rain heavily, so he hurried indoors with the sack of wood over his shoulder. It was such a night! The wind howled down the chimney, the rain lashed the windows, and the waves mounted the sea wall and flooded into the yard. He said a prayer for the fishermen out in their boats.

Just then, a wave hit the door with a crash and there was a plaintive cry from the outside. He opened the door and found a young seal lying on the doorstep. The little chap was brought in and revived by the fire. After that, they spent a merry evening together, and the unexpected guest drank John's milk, ate his fish supper and clapped its flippers while John played his mouth organ.

That night, John decided he should keep his new friend company in the kitchen, but he slept poorly. Each time he dozed off, he dreamed of a mother seal with tears streaming from her eyes—enough, he feared, to drown Cornwall, the British Isles and the whole world. He knew what he must do.

The assignment was not an easy one, however. They went to the beach together and there John picked up the youngster and waded out to deeper water, where he deposited his armful. However, the seal quickly turned and swam back to the beach. Several more tries were no more successful. So for the time being John conceded defeat and returned home with his friend.

They did not find a happy welcome. Sarah was there and she promptly advised, "Shoot the creature and I'll make it into a fur collar to wear on Sunday." That, however, John would never do, for he saw it as a child to be loved.

Each day, on their walks to the beach, John watched the waves, but the young seal kept its eyes on John. At last, up from the water, poked a shining head, looking each way.

"There's your mammy," said John. "So, my beauty, in you go!"

With that, he flung the youngster out as far as he could. He was relieved to hear the mother call and to see them join each other. He walked home, as lonely as he had ever been but pleased he had done what was right.

A week later, he walked again on the beach and started playing a hymn on his mouth organ. A moment later, the mother seal came to the surface with something round balanced on her nose. She tossed it into the air, caught it, and then sent it flying in John's direction.

He took it with both hands and discovered it was a small, round mirror framed by precious stones. Still more wonderful was what could be seen reflected in the mirror. Some bandy, pot-bellied old men lounging nearby appeared in the mirror to be noble and fit for heaven. He blushed to see his own reflection: calm, kind, majestic and beautiful.

So that everyone could get a new view of themselves, he fastened the mirror onto his front door. The villagers arrived giggling, shame-faced, fearful, impatient, jealous and angry. They left calm, confident, thoughtful of others, peaceful and with heads held high. One evening, a thief came to steal the jewels but saw himself as an angel, so he left quietly, for angels don't steal.

Sarah alone did not look into the mirror. She resented it because it had taken from her the pleasure of fault-finding. So early one morning, she approached it with her eyes closed, unhooked it and ran to the water's edge to return it to its original place. Standing on a large rock, she pitched it away from her. However, as it left her hand, for a split second, she caught sight of her reflection and cried out, "What have I done? I want it back!"

Just then, a shining head broke through the top of a wave. The mother seal caught the mirror on her nose, tossed it up once, caught it and sent it back over the waves to where Sarah was standing. However, there were tears in her eyes and the wind was blowing her hair across her face, and the mirror slipped through her fingers and shattered on the rocks at her feet.

After that, with no mirror to look into, most of the villagers returned to their old ways. Some, however, like John Pettigrew, kept a fragment of the broken mirror by them and carried in their hearts and minds a picture of the noble one they were meant to be.

Ruth Manning-Sanders, who wrote the story down, said that when she was a child she would sometimes become cross. It was then that her gentle old grandmother would shake her head and say, "Ah, child, you'd think differently if you could take a peep into John Pettigrew's mirror."

What might the story of John Pettigrew have been meant to teach readers/ listeners about themselves and others? Does it have significance for teachers?

---

1 The story here is adapted from "John Pettigrew's Mirror," written by Ruth Manning-Sanders. It appears in Denys Val Baker (editor), *One and All: A Selection of Stories from Cornwall* (London: Museum Press Limited, 1951), pages 270–282.

Believing is seeing

"If we wish to do good to souls, our success with these souls will be in proportion to their belief in our belief in, and appreciation of, them. Respect shown to the struggling human soul is the sure means through Christ Jesus of the restoration of the self-respect the man has lost. Our advancing ideas of what he may become is a help we cannot ourselves fully appreciate" (Ellen White, *Fundamentals of Christian Education*, page 281).

The above quote appeared in a manuscript titled "Suspension of students," dated 1893—two years after Ellen White reached Australia. Its message is plain: if I want to guide a struggling, wayward student, I must let them know that I believe they can make it. If they have lost their self-respect, we can help them by showing respect for them ourselves. The sooner we accept that, the more successful we will be in helping them.

I have in mind two boys—born within several years of each other. Both were of above average ability. Both were given the opportunity of college or university training and both took it up. One studied commerce and the other took on air-pilot training. One continued his interest in finance and became an investment banker. The other passed his flight training well, then turned around and took to driving taxis. I have no doubt that our passage for today holds much of the secret of the difference in the two outcomes—belief in oneself as encouraged by the home and the school.

There was once another boy born in a rough-hewn cabin, with an earth floor on which to walk. When he was nine years old, his mother died and his father was left to bring up two children. Thirteen months later, his father re-married and a stepmother, Sarah, moved in with her three children.

Sarah loved her stepchildren in the same way as she loved her own. She could see that the boy Abraham was intelligent, eager to do well and hard-working, and she encouraged him in every way possible. Starting with the Bible, *Aesop's Fables* and *Pilgrim's Progress,* which she brought with her, she opened up the wonders of reading, and then she encouraged him in writing and other studies. From time to time, Sarah would say to her stepson: "Be somebody, Abe."

Abraham Lincoln, who became perhaps the best-loved president of the United States, confessed, "All that I am, or hope to be, I owe to my angel mother."

We are all meant to be *somebody*. But who? Some time ago, this question was on the mind of a Jewish rabbi and philosopher called Zusya. One day, as he thought of the end of his life, Rabbi Zusya said, "In the coming world, they will not ask me, 'Why were you not Moses?' They will ask me, 'Why were you not Zusya?'"[1]

We may think about the students in our classes as unique, for that is what they all are. Who can comprehend what God has in store for them? We are to believe in them and, in quiet ways, let them know we have that belief. It may be that the respect we show them will strengthen their self-respect and point the way to their becoming the *somebody* God intends them to be.

Sooner or later, we will have students in our classes who are giving up hope that they will make the grade. What principles might we follow in relating to them?

---

1 Martin Buber, *Tales of the Hasidim: The Early Masters* (London: Thames and Hudson, 1956), page 251.

Hope that begets hope

"Looking upon them with hope, [Jesus] inspired hope. Meeting them with confidence, He inspired trust. Revealing in Himself man's true ideal, He awakened, for its attainment, both desire and faith" (Ellen White, *Education*, page 80).

On my desk, I have a rectangular piece of travertine stone, which I bought in Florence, Italy. I had two words carved on that stone, and both were used for teachers in ancient Rome, hundreds of years before the birth of Jesus.

On one side of the stone is carved the Latin word *magister*—the title given to one who stood or sat in front of a class and told students what they were to learn. To a *magister*, the class before him may have been no different from any other group he had taught before.

On the other side of the stone is the word *paedagogus*—the title given to one who took a personal interest in a particular student. A *paedagogus* was usually a slave who was given the responsibility of walking a child to school and sometimes sitting behind him to guide the child's behaviour and schoolwork. There is a famous use of the word *paidagogos* (the Greek form of the word) in Galatians 3:24, where the apostle Paul likened the law to this type of teacher.

These days, the idea behind the word *paedagogus* is used in an important way. When we want to talk about the best way to go about teaching a subject, we might speak of the principles of *pedagogy*—the art of teaching.

The three sentences at the head of this reading are about the way Jesus offered new life to those who had lost hope; however, they also relate to pedagogy—especially the teaching of students who may have lost hope of succeeding in school. Some of these students might have been taught by knowledgeable teachers, whether in mathematics, science, English, history or art. However, these teachers might not have known a lot about pedagogy. They might not have understood the difficulties that students have in mastering those subjects. They might have known little about how to stage the learning material so that the first steps are within reach and it is easy to move from one step to another. They might not have known how to make the subject full of interest, excitement and fun.

This is where you and I come in. Have our students learnt to trust us, believing we know the problems along the way and that we know how to tackle them one by one in a confident way? Do we look relaxed, as if we believe that what we are about to teach will be understood even by those who may be slower to catch on?

Let's apply our headline quote to classroom learning. If the look on our faces and our attitude are saying, "You can make it," then our confidence in our students may well inspire confidence in themselves. Hope will beget hope and we can look forward to their working diligently so they won't let us, or themselves, down.

That is the kind of teaching and learning that will give church schools the reputation they deserve.

Are there some further professional qualifications we could take in order to improve our pedagogy?

Is a student who is doing poorly in their schoolwork less likely to think seriously about their relationship with God?

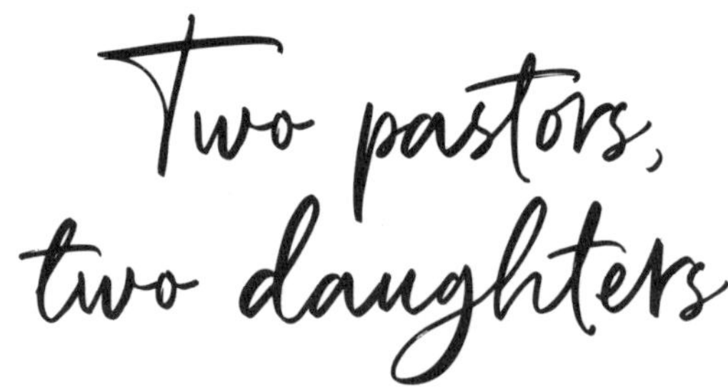

"I desire mercy, not sacrifice" (Hosea 6:6, NIV).

A large Adventist boarding school was served by a pastor who lived with his wife and family in a house at the gate of the school. Every person in the family was a baptised member of the church, as were a number of families in the surrounding village. This pastor had high standards and he lived by them in his home, at the school and at the church. The students knew about those standards and seemed willing to live up to them.

Then something tragic happened. The pastor's own daughter, in her late teens, became pregnant. With the whole school and the adult church members aware of the situation, the pastor wondered what he should do. In the end, he decided that his daughter should be made an example, and he led the church board to discipline her. This meant that her wrong-doing was written into the records of the church and for a time she could not hold any role in the church.

Soon after, the pastor moved on to another church, and a new pastor moved into the house by the school gate with his family. They too were all church members. And, sad to say, history repeated itself—the new pastor's unmarried eldest daughter became pregnant.

This time, the older women in the church took action for themselves. They knew their duty and arranged an interview with the young expectant mother. They had some questions to ask her—all of a similar kind. They asked what clothing she had for her coming little one. And did she have a cradle and baby carriage? Ninety women from the church gathered to reassure the mother-to-be and gave gifts for the coming arrival. Morning after morning, envelopes containing money were found at the front door of the house by the gate.

At the dedication of the child—a beautiful little boy—the pastor-grandfather remarked that although the little chap might never know his real daddy, he believed there were many in the congregation who would gladly fill in as part of the child's wider family. There was a chorus of "Amens" from the pews.[1]

In the difficult years ahead, there were occasions to think back on the tragedy of a date rape. Day by day, there were the struggles of sole parenting. Through it all, a church's refusal to condemn and determination to give loving support will bear a harvest to become fully evident only in eternity. And the student body was given a first-hand demonstration of mercy.

Some of us know the effect of fearing condemnation and finding loving support instead. F W Boreham told of a lad in church who nodded a few times, approaching sleep. He saw his father raise his hand and expected to be struck or shaken. Instead, the lad felt an arm placed around him, drawing him close to his father's side, where he rested with contentment. He remembered that bonding experience as long as he lived. I wonder if anyone has experienced that kind of mercy and support from us lately?

---

1 This story was told to the writer by the second pastor mentioned in this reading.

"[T]hrough love become slaves to one another....If, however, you bite and devour one another, take care that you are not consumed by one another" (Galatians 5:13, 15).

The story of Gudule starts in France in the year 1482.[1] She had been seduced, then forsaken, and she had to support herself as an unmarried mother. Her one joy was a beautiful child whom she called Agnes.

One day, a group of gypsies came to town and offered to tell the fortunes of children who were brought to them. Gudule took Agnes to see them and was told that the child would one day become a queen. Excited, she took Agnes home and laid her in her cot. As soon as the little one had fallen asleep, Gudule hurried to tell a neighbour the wonderful news of the future of her adorable daughter.

A few minutes later, Gudule returned and found the cot empty. She screamed in grief and searched about frantically. All she could find was a pink shoe lying on the floor. Later, she was told of two gypsy women who had been seen hurrying away carrying a small bundle. A search was made in all the lanes nearby, but the band of gypsies had left the district.

Fifteen years later, Gudule was living in a hide-away in the heart of Paris when her anger was roused by the arrival of a group of gypsies. She was especially furious at the sight of one of their band—a young dancing girl by the name of Esmeralda. Hardened and bitter from her tragic loss, Gudule would gladly have taken the girl's life as revenge for the kidnapping of her own Agnes, who would have been about Esmeralda's age.

Then her chance came. The little dancing girl was wrongly found guilty of murder and was left with Gudule until she was to be hanged. The bitter old woman fumbled at the clothing around her neck and brought out something tied to a ribbon. "Look!" she hissed at the prisoner. "This small shoe is all I have left of my beautiful child. Your people took her!"

At the sight of the shoe, Esmeralda trembled and whispered, "Wait!" Then she took hold of a little bag decorated with green beads that hung around her own neck. From this, she pulled out a small pink shoe. Attached to it was a piece of parchment with two lines inked onto it:

> Search till you find a match to this shoe;
> Your mother will stretch her hands out to you.

Feverishly, Gudule held the shoes side by side and found they matched perfectly. Then they fell into each other's arms—the one crying out, "My child!" and the other, "My mother!"

Unlikely as it might seem, resentment, bitterness and ill-feeling might sometimes be felt within a church school staffroom. Can we think of ways to prevent or deal with such a situation?

Applying our headline text for today could resolve many problems between teachers. In his letter to the Galatians, Paul gives us a vision of how God's children may best work together and let go of wrongs. In love, we are to "become slaves to one another." We are to look for ways to offer support—not finding fault with others or holding grudges against them.

In God's plan, the group of teachers in this present school has not been brought together by accident. When our gifts are lovingly placed beside someone else's gift (recall the two pink shoes), it might work wonders in converting resentment into happy cooperation. This change can happen in this school, in the local church community, and in the lives of our young people.

---

1 Gudule's story is adapted from the fictitious book *The Hunchback of Notre Dame* by Victor Hugo, which takes place mostly in Paris. The French pronunciation of Gudule is "Guh-DULE"—it sounds rather like "Good-Yule."

Power that heals

"Immediately aware that power had gone forth from him, Jesus turned about in the crowd and said, 'Who touched my clothes?'" (Mark 5:30).

"[T]hose who wait for the Lord shall renew their strength, they shall mount up with wings like eagles, they shall run and not be weary, they shall walk and not faint" (Isaiah 40:31).

As a child living in the hills behind Perth, Western Australia, I attended an Adventist *sole-charge* school—that is, a school where all the grades are taught by one teacher. For much of the time, there were no more than 20 pupils and my older brothers and I made up a fifth of the enrolment.

After training, I took my turn at teaching in Adventist sole-charge schools. These schools were in the island state of Tasmania and the enrolment was up to 35 students, spread over eight grades. It was tiring work.

While teaching there, I was visited from time to time by the Adventist director of education. He was a gifted teacher himself and had good counsel. During one of those visits, he gave me some important advice related to the text at the head of this reading. As teaching disciples of the Master Teacher and led by God's Spirit, he suggested that we also, in our small way, may relay power to students who reach out to us in our classes.

All well and good. However, we should be aware that there is a price to pay. Those who give themselves wholeheartedly to their students will experience a tiredness caused by more than standing on our feet for perhaps six hours a day. This relaying of power to our young people cannot be relieved by physical rest alone. It also requires spiritual renewal. The secret of finding that renewal has been known by God's servants for thousands of years. It involves a special kind of waiting.

John Bunyan, author of the famous *Pilgrim's Progress*, knew what it was to wait with God in prayer. After reading the beautiful words of Jeremiah 31:3, he longed to know that this love included himself, with all his mistakes and unworthiness. He paused and the words came back to him with sweet emphasis, "I have loved *thee* with an everlasting love."

On another morning, as he prayed, there came to his mind four precious words: "My grace is sufficient" (2 Corinthians 12:9). Each word was full of power. The "my" referred to none other than the omnipotent Ruler of the universe! And "grace"—it was there for the undeserving like him, who had let God down again and again. Then he thought of "sufficient"—not one whit less than what was needed to carry him through every trial that day![1] We too can find hope and strength in applying God's promises to our lives.

Having waited quietly on the Lord with meditations such as these, we may surely mount up like eagles, we may soar above daily trials, and we may relay heaven-sent power to those who reach out to us.

Shall we today follow Jesus' example in relating to those in His classes? "He watched the faces of His hearers, marked the lighting up of the countenance, the quick, responsive glace, which told that truth had reached the soul; and there vibrated in His heart the answering chord of sympathetic joy."[2] We too may know the response of "sympathetic joy," together with the relaying of heaven-sent power.

---

1 See John Bunyan, *Grace Abounding and the Life and Death of Mr Badman* (London: J M Dent, 1928), pages 60, 64, 65.

2 Ellen G White, *Education* (Mountain View, CA: Pacific Press Publishing Association, 1903), page 231.

Princess at the gate

"Rejoice always, pray without ceasing, give thanks in all circumstances" (1 Thessalonians 5:16–18).

"Take care that you do not despise one of these little ones; for, I tell you, in heaven their angels continually see the face of my Father in heaven" (Matthew 18:10).

"Let the little children come to me…for it is to such as these that the kingdom belongs" (Matthew 19:14).

Some years ago, after visiting a large public school, I was making my way out through the main gate towards my car. Several teachers and crowds of children were hurrying in the same direction. It was then that I saw a marvellous sight and knew I must stop.

There was a petite first-grader sitting on her lunchbox by a brick pillar. It was not her yellow rain-cape that caught my attention. Nor was it the golden ringlets falling about her face, nor the serious set of her lips. Rather, it was the fact that she was looking intently at a fine-print paperback copy of the New Testament.

A thousand might be passing at my side and ten thousand at my right hand, but still I must stop—for here, it seemed, was a child prodigy. Getting down to her eye level, I caught the five-year-old's attention and asked a silly question, "Can you read that?"

She replied with a gentle nod of the head, a faint smile and a softly spoken, "Yes."

With a smile for encouragement, I said, "Show me, would you?"

Without hesitating, she held the small book a little higher in both hands and, fixing her eyes on the page, she said in perfect intonation: "Thank you, God, for giving us *all* of the sky, and *all* of the trees, and *all* the food we need."

Her New Testament was open at Acts 8 and 9, and I don't know what Luke or Philip or Paul would have made of it, but for my part,

I was spellbound. When she lifted her eyes and looked into my face, I found myself nodding my head slightly and whispering, "Very good." And I still believe it.

Regardless of the scurrying feet and the bustle around her, our little five-year-old had been sitting in sweet communion with God. She knew she was holding God's Word in her hands. She knew she was welcome to reach out to God and speak with Him. Surely, "it is to such as these that the kingdom belongs" (Matthew 19:14).

This experience reminds me of something the preacher Charles Spurgeon once said. Referring to the words "my cup runneth over" in Psalm 23, Spurgeon wrote that if one is discontented, his cup will be cracked and leaking—it cannot run over.

Like the princess at the school gate, we need a contented and thankful heart. We can give thanks for the natural wonders around us, for the food we eat and the appetite to enjoy it. We can be thankful that we are loved and accepted by God and by our family and friends, and that He has given us His Word.

The apostle Paul was one of the most contented men of all time, and yet in some ways he was also greatly discontented. Compare, for example, 2 Corinthians 3:18, Philippians 4:11–13, Philippians 3:12–16 and Romans 15:23, 24. How can this difference be explained?

Thinking again of the princess at the school gate, what was there in her attitude that is a reminder of Jesus' words in Matthew 18:3, 4—that we are to "become like children" if we "are to enter the kingdom of heaven"?

Seeing the invisible

"[W]hat can be seen is temporary, but what cannot be seen is eternal" (2 Corinthians 4:18).

"[Moses] persevered as though he saw him who is invisible" (Hebrews 11:27).

During World War II, a company of Russian soldiers faced a similar number of German soldiers across an icy river. Both sides had heavy tanks but there was no bridge and no way to make a crossing. They knew that they would quickly be gunned down if they were seen building a bridge.[1] Day after day, the two sides watched each other, and nothing seemed to be happening.

Then a Russian engineer worked out a plan of attack. The parts of a bridge would be prepared during the day—out of sight. Then during the night, these parts would be put together under water without any lighting. An essential part of the plan was that the deck of the bridge was to be built 40 centimetres below the surface of the water—well out of sight.

On the other side of the river, the Germans sensed something was happening, but they could not tell what it was. They became more and more worried.

With the work complete, the engineers put in place a line of thin stakes to mark the path of the bridge. Then the Russian tank drivers were given their instructions and things were ready for the attack.

Watching from their side of the river, the Germans were puzzled to see the Russian tanks gathering on the opposite bank. They saw the first tank make its way down the riverbank and enter the water. To their horror, the tank did not sink but made its way across the river in their direction. With the enemy unprepared, other tanks followed and the battle was soon won.

There is something interesting here. The lives of the Russian tank drivers and their crews depended on something they could not see, either in the darkness of night or in the light of day. But they knew that it was real and that it was there.

One of our texts for today suggests that this situation would not have surprised Moses as he led his difficult bunch of students through the wilderness. Every day, he persevered, believing in what he could not see with his two natural eyes. The things Moses could see—like the wilderness saltbushes and the desert sands that beat in his face—were only temporary. However, God's presence and the heavenly Canaan prepared for His children were real.

With that kind of vision—trusting in the One we cannot see—our battles will surely be won.

Could the promise given by God in Exodus 33:14 have led Moses to persevere "as though he saw him who is invisible"? Moses regarded this promise as making his people "distinct" (verse 16). For those of God's children today who accept this same promise, what can we suggest would be distinctive about the way we "persevere"?

---

1 The story is adapted from a set of readers authored by the present writer in the early 1980s.

Birds of prey

"And when birds of prey came down on the carcasses,
Abram drove them away" (Genesis 15:11).

"Watch as faithfully as did Abraham lest the ravens or any
birds of prey alight upon your sacrifice and offering to God"
(Ellen White, *Selected Messages*, Book 2, page 243).

It was a solemn day in the life of Abram. Years before, he had responded to the call to leave the luxury of his home in Ur in ancient Sumeria and to go wherever God should lead him. He first went north-west between the rivers to Haran, then south-west to Canaan—destined to own no dwelling but a tent.

And now the Lord was to make a covenant with him—a promise of an expanse of the middle-eastern world. However, first Abram was to make a sacrifice of three choice animals from his flock and of two birds. He cut the animals in two and laid them out with the birds, leaving a pathway between the pieces.

The sight was enough to attract the birds of prey, which began to circle above. However, as often as they alighted on the pieces, the patriarch was there to beat them away. He did not forget that these animals were his offering to the Lord and that no creature should tear them apart.

With the sun sinking below the horizon, Abram drifted into a deep sleep and a "terrifying darkness" settled upon him. Then he was reassured as the voice of the Lord spelled out the future of his descendants.

In the darkness, Abram watched in awe as a mysterious demonstration took place. Two objects came into view—a fire-pot with smoke streaming from it and a blazing torch—making a journey between the pieces of his offering. He could not help but notice that no visible hand suspended the pot and that the torch seemed to move without anyone to hold it. As in his own life, the guidance was unseen but sure.

Like Abram, our lives and service have been placed in God's hands. We too may know that unseen hands are guiding our daily witness. Like the apostle Paul, we can remind ourselves and each other that the things that can presently be seen are but temporary. It is "what cannot be seen [that] is eternal" (2 Corinthians 4:17, 18).

This story makes another point, and it is found in the texts at the head of our story today. Like Abram, we too have been called to make an offering—a "living sacrifice, holy and acceptable to God" and this is at the heart of our "spiritual worship" (Romans 12:1). How tragic if "the ravens or any birds of prey" should alight upon it and devour it!

Here is something I find quite interesting. We first come across the name of Abram towards the end of Genesis 11. At the beginning of that chapter, we are told of the builders of the tower of Babel. They said to each other: "Come, let us build ourselves a city, and a tower with its top in the heavens, and let us make a name for ourselves" (Genesis 11:4). Those city-builders failed miserably and no-one knows their names. On the other hand, Abram left the luxury of the city and lived in a tent for the remainder of his life. His name is well-known around the globe—with more than half the world's population regarding him as their spiritual forebear. His commitment to protecting his offering bore fruit.

What "birds of prey" might threaten our sense of personal sacrifice and commitment? Envy of our fellow teachers, resentment of what we see as unfair criticism or the favouring of other staff members? Discovery of failures in the lives of those in leadership? What else?

How might we best drive off the birds of prey that could come to spoil our sacrifice? We do well to keep in mind that at times we might need a change of heart towards others. At other times, we could follow the principles given in Matthew 18:15–17. Extremities may require advice from the school principal and may call for the setting up of a grievance committee.

China follows "the blueprint"

"Schools should be established that, in addition to the highest mental and moral culture, shall provide the best possible facilities for physical development and industrial training" (Ellen White, *Education*, pages 214, 218).

"Moral, intellectual, and physical culture should be combined in order to have well-developed, well-balanced men and women" (Ellen White, *Counsels to Teachers, Parents and Students*, page 290).

In 1914, 17-year-old Denton Rebok enrolled at Washington Missionary College, set on becoming a medical doctor. However, God had other plans and young Denton was willing to follow wherever they might lead.[1]

During his studies, he met Florence Kneeland, born of missionary parents in British Guiana—since 1966, the independent nation of Guyana—in the Caribbean. She shared Denton's hopes and commitment, and they were married after his graduation in May, 1917.

The young couple was known to the Mission Board of the General Conference of Seventh-day Adventists and they were soon given a call to work in China. In early August, they boarded the *Empress of Russia* in Vancouver, bound for Yokohama, Japan, then Hong Kong. After a short delay, they reached the coastal city of Swatou, in the Chinese province of Kwangtung. There they were greeted warmly by a fellow American, Pastor J P Anderson, and a Chinese pastor, Ang Tsz-kieh, who took the newcomers to the mission station perched on the bank of the river. The Reboks were barely out of their teens but were determined to take up their work happily and faithfully.

After a year, Denton and Florence had made a good start on learning the Chinese language and the local customs. Denton was made a departmental director—in charge of the publishing and educational work of the South China Union—and soon after, he was given his most difficult assignment since reaching China. Elder I H Evans, president of the China Division, asked him to set up and administer the church's first training college in China. He was to choose the teachers, find the students and settle on the location.

There were already Christian colleges in China. Should he follow them as a pattern? It would be easy enough to do so. Instead, he went to three of Ellen White's books written for Adventist schools around the globe. There was *Education*, published in 1903. Then there were *Counsels to Teachers, Parents and Students* and *Fundamentals of Christian Education,* both published in 1913, along with articles selected from other Adventist publications. Denton's reading showed him that a Christian school should not only be concerned with the mind of the student but also with the heart and the hands. In God's plan, they were all to be developed.

He quickly discovered that such a broad approach was not going to be easy in China in the 1920s. Scholars there were expected to use their minds but never their hands for physical labour. They walked about slowly in long robes with their hands hidden in long sleeves.

After much hard work, the Shanghai Missionary College opened its doors, and Denton was ready to tackle the matter of physical activity. He had the college teachers play a friendly game of football, with the students invited to watch. Soon they wanted to join in, and it was not long before both faculty and students were enjoying vigorous exercise every day—in trousers rather than robes.

Then Denton introduced the students to manual work. He did not tell them to start doing tasks around the college. Instead, he took two of the young men with him as he cleaned the toilets, a task that needed to be completed every day. As expected, they were disgusted that the president of the college would do such lowly work.

On the third day, one of the students, Liu Chi-cheng, said, "Sir, you are the president of the college?"

"Yes," he replied, "I am the president."

"And can the president of the college do this kind of work? It is such menial work."

"It needs to be done, so it is honourable. And if it is honourable, it is good enough for the president of the college to do. So let's get it done quickly and as well as we can."

Liu held out his hand for the bucket, saying, "If the president can do it, we can too." The same young man later went on to medical college and worked for a good number of years as a surgeon.

Denton's next move was to set up college industries so that the students could work to pay their fees. It wasn't easy going; however, they eventually produced bed frames, school desks, library equipment and chairs. Their customers included Nanking University, a girls' school and a nearby hospital. In their second year of production, their sales to the university alone reached $400,000.[2]

With his mind still on the blueprint given in Ellen White's three books, Denton had a final project to achieve. The college should be moved to a country setting. Nobody had ever seen it done before. However, land was bought in Jiangsu province, 257 kilometres (160 miles) from Shanghai, 48 kilometres (30 miles) from Nanking, in view of the Yangtze River. In 1925, after long months of hard work, the China Training Institute was ready to commence its important work of preparing young people to serve the church and the surrounding community. In that year, Denton Rebok had his 28th birthday.[3]

What do you see as the secret of Denton Rebok's success? Would it still work today?

There is much to be gained from following Denton Rebok's example in reading the three books from which he took the blueprint for his work. Staff members may wish to work together to read through these books, along with Testimonies for the Church, Volume 6 *(perhaps dividing up the reading). In the process, it might be valuable to discuss whether there are blueprint features that could be given more emphasis in this school.*

1 The account given here is adapted from Herbert Ford, *For the Love of China: The Life Story of Denton E Rebok* (Mountain View, CA: Pacific Press Publishing Association, 1971), commencing with page 37.

2 This value, quoted from the source above, is presumably the then US-dollar equivalent of the original sum.

3 After 23 years in China, Denton Rebok returned to the United States where he taught religion at Washington Missionary College. Later, he was appointed president of Southern Junior College, in Tennessee; president of the Seventh-day Adventist Theological Seminary; chairman of the E G White Publications Board; and secretary of the General Conference of Seventh-day Adventists. His postgraduate studies commenced with a master's degree at the University of Nanking and concluded with a doctoral degree at Columbia University in New York. He died in 1983.

When champions meet

"[W]ho is this uncircumcised Philistine that he should defy the armies of the living God?" (1 Samuel 17:26).

"[L]ooking to Jesus...who for the joy that was set before him endured the cross, despising the shame" (Hebrews 12:2).

Historically, the word "champion" had a special meaning. A champion was someone whose achievements counted as being carried out by all their followers. The giant Goliath acted as the champion of the Philistines at the valley of Elah, and he called for Israel to name a champion of their own to represent them in battle:

> Choose a man for yourselves, and let him come down to me. If he is able to fight with me and kill me, then we will be your servants; but if I prevail against him and kill him, then you shall be our servants and serve us (1 Samuel 17:9).

The handsome young David arrived in the midst of this drama, fresh from shepherding on the hillsides of Bethlehem. He was outraged that an "uncircumcised Philistine" had "defied the armies of the living God" (1 Samuel 17:26) and surprised that no-one in the camp of Israel had come forward to meet Goliath in battle. Not the king. Not one of the captains. Not one of the shepherd boy's warrior brothers. It was more than the young lion-and-bear-slayer could tolerate, and he decided to step into the gap himself.

David's visible means of support didn't appear to be great. He had no more than any Hebrew shepherd boy carried by way of equipment—a staff, a sling, five smooth stones and a pouch in which to carry them. However, his invisible means of support was second to none—it included a sense of God's unfailing presence, a practised dependence on God's leading and a willingness to put total effort into his daily tasks, whether they be humdrum or earth-shaking.

The two combatants had their say and then approached each other. The giant came on ponderously, moving under the weight of a cartload of heavy metal, while David sprinted forward lightly, carrying a weapon of unsuspected power. The Philistine champion assumed the battle would be over in minutes. The visor on his helmet was thrown back, the better to relish the carving up of an insignificant adversary.

The spectators on either side of the valley stood riveted to the spectacle being acted out before their eyes. This was no ordinary contest—they were watching as one champion faced another. Within seconds, one whole army would enjoy the fruits of victory and the other would become bond-servants.

Quickly, a stone was fitted into the pocket of the shepherd's sling. Then, with arm and eyes well practised in the fields of Bethlehem, David aimed the stone at Goliath's exposed forehead. The missile did its intended work and the stricken champion fell, measuring out his "six cubits and a span" (1 Samuel 17:4) on the Elah turf. David administered the final stroke with Goliath's own sword.

A thousand years later, another Champion walked Planet Earth—the One to whom all previous Hebrew champions were intended to point. Like David, this Champion too was born in Bethlehem. If He won the battle, evil would be doomed forever. The chief-giant, the enemy of God's people throughout time, knew this all too well and it terrified him. Working through men, the enemy plotted to destroy God's Champion at Calvary.

But like Goliath of old, the chief-enemy had miscalculated his Adversary. He did not understand the weapon used against him. Jesus, the anointed Champion,

> did not regard equality with God as something to be exploited, but emptied himself, taking the form of a slave, being born in human likeness. And being found in human

> form, he humbled himself and became obedient to the point of death—even death on a cross (Philippians 2:5–8).

The glory of God—the ultimate demonstration of love—was seen not through brute force but through self-sacrificing love for a rebellious and ungrateful race. Satan's claims against God were proved false and the price for human sin was paid. The battle was won for all of us through our Champion, Jesus.

The achievements of a champion belong to those who stand with him. Do we identify with the Servant-King? Are His values ours? Then His victory is ours as well.

What was David's preparation for his victory in the valley of Elah? Does it have anything to guide us in our daily teaching commitment?

The gates that could not prevail

"[U]pon this rock I will build my church; and the gates of hell shall not prevail against it" (Matthew 16:18, KJV).

"I am he that liveth, and was dead; and, behold, I am alive for evermore, Amen; and have the keys of hell and of death" (Revelation 1:18, KJV).

It was night-time in the city of Gaza. Samson, the most physically powerful of all the Hebrew judges, was inside the city and the Philistines knew it. The gates were closed and locked to keep the strongman in until the morning, when his enemies planned to slay him.[1]

At midnight, Samson approached the gateway and found his way barred. He had no key to undo the locks and no silver to bribe the gatekeeper. But he had another way out. The gates of this miniature city of hell would not prevail against God's champion.

He reached out and grasped the pillars on which the gates were hinged and jostled them in their sockets. Then he stooped and lifted the gates—pillars and all—onto his back and shoulders. Carrying the gates intended to hold him prisoner, Samson marched towards the top of a neighbouring hill. Perhaps he turned in the moonlight to survey the results of his work. The gap in the wall of this wounded city would have stood out like a missing front tooth. Anyone trapped inside the city was free to come out.

Many years later, John, the longest-living of all the apostles, was imprisoned on the island of Patmos. (It is 30 kilometres [20 miles] off the coast of modern Turkey.) One Sabbath day, he was taken into vision by God's Spirit. He no longer heard the sound of the waves washing in from the Aegean Sea; rather, he heard a thrilling trumpet-like voice: "I am he that liveth, and was dead; and, behold, I am alive for evermore, Amen; and have the keys of hell and of death" (Revelation 1:18, KJV).

Jesus' words signify His power to unlock the prison-house of the grave and give unending life to those who identify with Him. The gates of hell cannot prevail against God's church; neither can they triumph against the Lord of the church.[2] It might be said that the priceless keys to hell and death were in the lock of the door waiting for humankind's Champion to claim them from the inside. This, no-one else could do.

Recall that when Samson prevailed against the gates of ancient Gaza, he left a gaping hole in the walls of his prison-house. So it is for us today: the Strongman of eternity holds the long-hoped-for keys to the prison-house of death. Now all who accept Jesus as their Champion may march out in joyful triumph.

Suppose someone approaches you as a Christian teacher and asks what they must do to be counted as a child of God and have Jesus as their Champion. What would you say to them?

---

1 The story is told in Judges 16:2, 3.

2 The expression "the gates of hell" may have more than one meaning. It could refer to the fact that the forces of evil will never be able lock in our Lord or His church—their escape is always going to be possible. Then there is the meaning gained from understanding the role of the gates of a city in the Old Testament. A good Bible dictionary will advise that the area around the city gates was a main legal, business and civic centre. This could be suggesting that all the plotting and planning of the evil powers will not succeed in overpowering God's church. The present worship readings concentrate on the former of these two.

The power of love versus the love of power

"Love is patient; love is kind; love is not envious or boastful or arrogant or rude. It does not insist on its own way; . . . it does not rejoice in wrongdoing, but rejoices in the truth" (1 Corinthians 13:4–6).

Gottfried Oosterwal was born on February 8, 1930, and spent his early years in the city of Rotterdam in the Netherlands. His parents were Adventists and met each Sabbath with a group of church members for Bible study and worship. Because they could not afford a church building, they rented the basement of a bicycle shop. It was a happy, close-knit church family. The adults would call Gottfried, "Bobby," and he would call them "Aunty" and "Uncle." The church family often visited in each other's homes around the city.[1]

Bobby's friends showed him where they went to church. The buildings were large and grand. Sometimes they would ask to see where he went to church. He would say, "Oh, I wouldn't bother."

On Sabbaths, when his family would walk to church, he was afraid his school friends might see him, so he would run ahead to get to the bicycle shop as quickly as possible. His parents would sometimes say to their friends, "Bobby loves church so much he can't get there fast enough!"

After school, Bobby and his friends would sometimes roam around the city together. If it was hot, one of them might ask, "Bobby, do you have any aunts or uncles near here?" Then he would take them to the home of one of the Adventist families and ask for a drink. None of his friends were comfortable to drop in on members of their own churches like that. Bobby began to realise that what his little church lacked in buildings, it made up for in being a loving family.

Friday, May 10, 1940, was a sadly memorable day for the Dutch people. With war heating up in other parts of Europe, the German airforce and army set about taking over the Netherlands. Rotterdam, with its shipping links, was an early target. Paratroopers came down swiftly. The invasion was quite visible from the Oosterwal home.

The following morning was Sabbath and, although the Germans were still making secure their hold on the city, Bobby's mother dressed her children for church. His father was concerned for his family's safety, but, encouraged by his wife's faith, they all set out to walk the necessary distance. Telling of the experience 50 years later, Bobby spoke of the way he walked to church that day with a new feeling in his heart. Instead of being worried his friends might see him going to his humble church, he felt proud that he was part of a family that took its religion seriously enough to brave the streets while armed paratroopers were standing at the intersections. His father explained to the sentries where they were going and eventually they were allowed to pass.

Three days later, the main part of Rotterdam was largely flattened by bombs. Within the week, ground troops had moved in and the whole country was under German control. Resistance was pointless by then and the Dutch people had to accept their occupied status.

Something unforgettable took place on Sabbath, May 25. As the Adventist church family was meeting in the basement of the bicycle shop as usual, they heard the sound of heavy boots descending the staircase. Then the door opened and a uniformed German soldier stood there looking from one to another. No-one said a word.

At last, Bobby saw the head deacon go to speak to the intruder. Trembling with resentment, he spoke tensely, "Why have you come? You ruin our city. You destroy our homes. You take away our livelihood. And now you come and interrupt our church service. Go away and leave us alone!"

Everyone watched to see what the German soldier would do. He did not move. Instead, he looked calmly at the head deacon and at the family of worshippers. Then he said quietly, "I am a Seventh-day Adventist, and I have come to worship with you. I am your brother."

The church family saw the head deacon swallow hard and look at the uniformed soldier with a new expression. They watched as he came close to the newcomer and placed an arm around him. Then he spoke with emotion, "Yes—if you have come to worship, you are our brother." Then he led him to the front seat and sat with him for the remainder of the service.

This incident is an illustration of the difference between the two attitudes referred to in the title of today's reading: the love of power and the power of love. Above ground level, no-one would have doubted that the *excluding* love of power was the clear winner in Rotterdam in 1940. Yet, in one little basement corner, something else was happening—the *including* power of love was shining through, as it will in Earth's final struggle.

We are not pre-programmed robots. We have been given the right to choose, and we are daily given the opportunity to throw in our lot with one side or the other. We may join the way of the one who first hungered for power (see Isaiah 14:13) or we may choose to follow Jesus' example and live by the power of love. If we choose Jesus' way, we will value others as God values them, as demonstrated on Calvary's hill long ago. And that is a good reason why eternity, in the Earth made new, will be forever safe.

Using the power of love in the classroom does not mean, of course, that we are weak and indecisive in correction of wrongdoing and in showing the standard of work and behaviour we expect. The timid—and even those not so timid—want to see teachers who are in control of the classroom and playground. A sense of trust and confidence is ideal for both the blossoming of personality and the mastery of classwork. What signs are our students likely to look for in deciding whether we are relating to them and others under the power of love or under the love of power?

---

1 The account given here is adapted from the story as told by Dr Oosterwal on two occasions in the city of Sydney. Much of it was also published in G Oosterwal, "The day I became proud to be an Adventist," *Adventist Professional*, Vol 1, No 1, not dated, pages 11–14.

In quietness comes strength

"In returning and rest you shall be saved; in quietness and in trust shall be your strength. . . . [Y]our eyes shall see your Teacher. And when you turn to the right or when you turn to the left, your ears shall hear a word behind you, saying, 'This is the way; walk in it'" (Isaiah 30:15, 20, 21).

A certain father was worried about his son, who was halting in his speech, timid and struggling with his schoolwork. He was a tall, well-built man—a gentle giant. He went to see the school principal and told him the situation. The principal said, "Let's go and talk with his teacher." They were almost at the classroom door when they heard the teacher use the boy's family name impatiently, saying, "We can't wait all day to listen to you!" The principal quickly opened the door and exclaimed, "His father is here!" And he certainly was, looking imposing as his large frame almost filled the doorway.

I heard the story when the father brought the boy to the Adventist school where I was principal. We had the opportunity to show what can happen when teachers believe that students can be confident of our respect and support, whether they do well or poorly.

In our plans for each day, we can work and pray for a quietness in our students' hearts that makes way for God to speak to each member of the class. Such a quietness is born of trust—for example, when the student knows the teacher will be patient, kind and fair. It makes a difference when students know that the teacher will not try to embarrass them and that they can feel secure in the learning environment we provide. There is a quietness in the hearts of those who feel secure and confident. They are not in fear of the ridicule of others—be it the teacher or their classmates.

In fact, I know of some teachers who respond to disturbances in class by lowering their voice rather than raising it. It is easier for a student to grasp that their teacher values them when their name is spoken quietly and confidingly—even in correction.

The gospel prophet, Isaiah, is clear that we have a Teacher worthy of our quiet trust. We are to see Him and hear Him every day and allow Him to save us, strengthen us and guide our actions. He is, indeed, "not far from each one of us" (Acts 17:27).

I am confident that the direction and re-direction of the rest of one's life can take place in these moments of quietness between God and the student—when the Holy Spirit speaks and the student hears and is convinced that the Lord is God and that He has a claim on their personal lives. I am confident of this because it happened to me as a teenager—in an Adventist college.

Our text for this morning tells us that "in quietness and in trust shall be your strength." What makes a quiet trust so effective in spiritual and mental renewal?

First avenue to learning

"His heart was crying, How can I give thee up? The constraining power of that love was felt by Judas. When the Saviour's hands were bathing those soiled feet, and wiping them with the towel, the heart of Judas thrilled through and through with the impulse then and there to confess his sin" (Ellen White, *Desire of Ages*, page 645).

Teachers need to talk and demonstrate, and students need to listen and watch. To find out how much they know, we may also get them to speak and to write. This method of education has been followed for thousands of years and has produced some good results. But it is not the only way to learn. Nor is it the first way we learn or, at times, the best way.

In God's plan, touch is an important teaching and learning tool. The Creation story in Genesis 2 tells us that human life commenced when the Creator came close and breathed into the nostrils of His new child. From that first physical touch, humans were to understand that the One who rules over all matter, space and time also loves us tenderly. Likewise, in the Upper Room, when Jesus bathed the feet of His disciples, the touch of His hands told so much of the love He had for each of them. As the passage at the head of today's reading suggests, Jesus' touch almost led Judas to confess and turn from his sin.

When a child is born, it is touch that gives the infant their earliest sensations of security, nourishment and love. "Skin hunger"—the desire for physical closeness—is the signal that human touch is meant to be a blessing for as long as we live—for the breastfed newborn, for the growing infant, for the child and the adolescent, and for those in the exclusive domain of married life. Even in the simple act of shaking hands, we convey a lot about how much we value each other.

It may be that young people have a special gift for knowing what a touch means. Some years ago, I was visiting a Northern Hemisphere classroom. The class teacher was there and maybe two dozen children, and I had permission to speak with them. I sat down beside a beautiful dark-skinned, curly-headed, nine-year-old boy and asked what he liked and didn't like about school. He told me that one thing that saddened him was when teachers ask how you are, then they just rumple your hair and keep going.

Touch is not only important for learning about and building relationships, it helps with classroom studies as well. The point can be illustrated from a story told by the Italian-American educator and motivational speaker, Felice Leonardo Buscaglia (1924–1998).[1] As a beginning pupil, he came on well with a loving teacher whom he trusted and loved in return. A little later, he had a teacher who was not so understanding. On one occasion she gave the lad a note for his immigrant mother, complaining that her son was "too tactile." Her ever-present dictionary let her know that tactile was about feeling and touching. At this, she exclaimed, "So what's a-wrong with that? That's a-nice. You gotta crazy teacher."

A teaching degree is not always essential for understanding the maxim: What I touch and handle and do, I understand and remember and apply to new situations.

Jean Piaget (1896–1980), probably the best-known child psychologist of the 20th century,[2] emphasised the importance of learners having "concrete" objects in their hands. He emphasised that this allowed them to think logically about those objects as they moved them around. They could also form pictures and models in their minds of the things they touched and felt.

Watch a two-year-old looking at decorations on a Christmas tree. They must go over and gently tip those shiny coloured balls with their fingers—or better still hold one in the palm of their hand. With the mind well furnished with such experiences, thinking could be described as actions carried out in the mind with those inner models—that is a large part of thinking and problem-solving.

Pity the adolescent with an impoverished tactile childhood. In their mathematics assignments, in their geography textbooks, and in their English and History classes, words will lack richness of meaning. It is the work of the gifted teacher to provide "structured" materials that the student can handle—materials that can illustrate and model the processes that are being taught.

The ideas of Jean Piaget were spelt out further by an Italian-American, Professor Jerome Bruner (1915–2016). He advised that, in guiding the learner, we do well to have them move through three stages, which we can refer to as Doing (with the hands), Picturing (on paper and in the mind), and Representing (for example, in speech and with numbers and operation signs).[3] Teachers wanting to follow these stages with their learners take care to commence with handling or moving about real objects. Examples might include wooden blocks for teaching squares of numbers; coins and bank notes for teaching interest; clay modelled in a waterproof tray for introducing contour maps, or depositing and withdrawing money from a simulated bank for teaching positive and negative numbers.

The school principal may wish to set aside some time in a staff meeting in which teachers can mention topics they are planning to introduce to their classes, giving other teachers opportunity to suggest structured material that could be brought to class for the students to handle, helping them build new inner models for their thinking.

---

1 Dr Buscaglia's first given name is pronounced "FEEL-i-chay" and his family name is pronounced "bus-CARL-yuh." The piece of dialogue given here is from his book, *Living, Loving and Learning* (London: Souvenir Press, 1983, page 228.

2 Professor Piaget's given name Jean is the French form of John. It can be pronounced "zyuh." His family name has the emphasis on the final syllable: pee-uh-ZYAY.

3 In his book, *The Process of Education* (Cambridge, MA: Harvard University Press, 1960), Jerome Bruner titles these stages Enactive, Iconic and Symbolic.

Training the physical abilities

"It is in the order of God that the physical as well as the mental powers shall be trained" (Ellen White, *Counsels to Parents, Teachers and Students*, page 281).

"Moral, intellectual, and physical culture should be combined in order to have well-developed, well-balanced men and women" (Ellen White, *Counsels to Parents, Teachers and Students*, page 290).

All young people are different, but some especially stand out. It was that way with Helen Keller.

She was born in the American state of Alabama on June 27, 1880, and after a severe illness at 19 months of age, she was left both deaf and blind. Unable to hear, she was not able to speak either.[1]

Being a bright and inquisitive child, Helen used her remaining senses to discover and enjoy the world around her. She soon managed to feel her way along a hedge near her home and find, by their perfume, the violets coming into bloom. She found comfort in hiding her face in the grass and leaves in the nearby fields.

In the summer months of 1886, the family travelled by train to Baltimore and then to Washington DC, where they met Dr Alexander Graham Bell, whose mother and wife were both deaf. Dr Bell helped Helen's parents to find a teacher for her. Her name was Anne Sullivan and she arrived a few days before she turned 21, and a few months before Helen turned seven. As an adult, Helen described that day as "the most important day I remember in all my life." She described the meeting like this:

> I felt approaching footsteps. I stretched out my hand as I supposed to my mother. Some one (sic) took it, and I

> was caught up and held close in the arms of her who had come to reveal all things to me, and, more than all things else, to love me.

The learning of words started the next day. A doll was placed in her hands to play with for a while. Then the letters "d-o-l-l" were spelled out into her hand. The same with *pin, cup* and *hat* and some verbs such as *sit, stand* and *walk*. All this time, Helen enjoyed the finger play but she did not understand it as giving her names for these things and actions. This she learnt a few days later when Anne Sullivan led her outside where someone was using a water pump. As Helen felt the water splashing over one hand, the letters "w-a-t-e-r" were spelled out into the other hand, slowly at first, then quickly. Suddenly, the miracle of language came to life. "That living word awakened [her] soul, gave it light, hope, joy, set it free!"

She realised there was a name for everything she could touch and for everything she could do! Word after word was added that day—*mother*, *father*, *sister*, *teacher*—and many others. And with each new word came something new for thinking about and making further inquiries.

Again and again, the young Helen came to know her world through what she could touch and feel. She could not hear a cat purring or a dog bark; however, with her arms about them, she could feel these things happening. She could not see the mighty Niagara Falls, but when standing near on the overhanging rocks, she was thrilled to "[feel] the air vibrate and the earth tremble." Many of us will never know the intensity of such feelings.

Through the years, Helen shook hands with hundreds of people, and by this means she often learnt more about them than others who were able to see and hear. From the touch of their hands, she knew when she was meeting people who had no joy in their lives. There were others, she decided, "whose hands have sunbeams in them." Some people's touch imparted a heavenly restfulness and a sense of healing. After learning to tell what a speaker was saying by touching their lips, she "heard" Mark Twain tell some of his great stories. She could "feel the twinkle of his eye" in his handshake.

While still a child, she loved to sit on Bishop Brooks' knee, clasping "his great hand" with one of hers while her teacher "spelled into the other his beautiful words about God and the spiritual world." From him, she learned about the "key to Heaven"—loving God and "every child of God" and remembering that "the possibilities of good are greater than the possibilities of evil."

Helen Keller's story is a reminder of a special responsibility placed upon us as church school teachers. The references at the head of this reading bid us to think of ways in which young people can be guided in developing their physical abilities. Games are meant to be lots of fun and can be when the hands and feet and eyes are being co-ordinated in better ways. Crafts and the handling of tools are often neglected these days. A 17-year-old working at a sewing machine or handling a saw can be seen as working towards the same objectives as a five-year-old threading beads on a string or a six-year-old tying a bow. All are demonstrating that the physical is being trained along with the intellectual, emotional and spiritual facets of their lives.

Dr Maria Montessori, whom we met earlier, had some frames made that very young children could use to practise physical tasks—things like tying a bow; doing up buttons, press studs and zippers; and buckling a buckle. Can we think of other physical skills that could be trained, perhaps in conjunction with the home, including skills of interest to teenagers? Using a potter's wheel could prove popular. How about bed-making, ironing clothes and cookery for both young men and young women?

---

1 Most of the details given in this reading are adapted from Helen Keller, *The Story of My Life* (New York: Dover Publications, 1996). The original publication was in 1903 by Doubleday, Page and Co.

Shay and the "grand slam"

"Come unto me, all you that are weary and are carrying heavy burdens, and I will give you rest" (Matthew 11:28).

Shay had always found his studies difficult, so he was placed in a special school for the handicapped in Brooklyn, New York. He knew why he was there and he looked on other teenage boys with a sense of sad loneliness.[1]

One afternoon, he and his dad were out walking. Soon they came upon a park where some boys about Shay's age were playing baseball. He turned to his father and said, "Would they let me join in, do you think?"

His father knew that Shay had never played baseball and that he understood almost nothing about the game. However, he loved his son and decided to ask, even though he expected a refusal. He spoke to one of the nearby boys, asking if his son could join in even for a few minutes. The lad looked at Shay and summed up the situation promptly.

"Yes," he said. "When we go out next, he can take my place in right field. We're losing, but he might get a chance to bat in our last innings."

Soon the team went out to the field, and Shay with them, proudly wearing a fielder's glove. He had no idea what he was meant to do, but he was there with the other boys. His father saw him smiling as never before.

Then Shay's side came back in to bat. To everyone's surprise, several players managed to get the ball away and get home. Finally, with two batters out and the bases loaded, they could actually win if the next batter could hit a home run. And it was Shay's turn.

His father, watching from the sidelines, expected that a substitute batter would be called upon. But, no. They called Shay to the plate, showed him where to stand and put a bat in his hands.

Everyone could see that he had never hit a ball in his life. So the pitcher stepped off his mound, walked half way to the batter and tossed the ball up softly. Shay didn't move. Two more pitches to go.

The pitcher came still closer and tossed the ball up again. Shay's side shouted, "Swing!" He swung, but nowhere near the ball. One more pitch to go.

Just then, the boy who had given his place to Shay came over and showed him how to hold the bat. The last pitch came in and somehow he managed to touch the ball and it dribbled towards the pitcher. The pitcher had plenty of time to throw it to first base and finish the game.

But, no, again. He threw the ball high—beyond first base, into right field. Everyone shouted, "Run, Shay, run. Go to first." And gasping desperately, that is what the handicapped lad did.

The player in right field now had the chance to send the ball to second base so that Shay could be tagged out. However, he too sent a high throw over the base-man's head.

Everyone shouted, "Go, Shay! Go to second!"

As soon as he arrived, the shortstop of the fielding side turned him around and pointed to third base.

"Third!" both teams screamed. And then, "Home, Shay, home!"

Tiring now, Shay half hobbled to the home plate. Realising that somehow, in his first game, his son had managed a "grand slam" and that he would have something joyful to remember as long as he lived, his father found his face bathed in tears.

Just as important: both teams had demonstrated that there are some things more important than winning a game.

Why did the teenage baseball players in today's reading behave in the heroic way we have considered? If they were asked, they would hardly have used language like choosing "the power of love" over "the love of power." However, their words might well have a similar meaning—for example: "It was the only decent thing we could do" or "He had it coming to him—he's suffered enough."

There are many classrooms and schools with one or more students evidently different in some way. How are they treated in our schools—schools that carry the names Adventist and Christian? Are they included and nurtured or are they excluded and bullied? Is there anything more we could do to help these students experience the rest from their burdens that Jesus promised?

---

1 The story is adapted from "The Day Shay Got To Play" by E J Nolan, found online at <https://www.baseball-almanac.com/poetry/po_shay.shtml>. A companion musical rendition is also given.

Teller of stories wins Lake Titicaca

"I make it my ambition to proclaim the good news, not where Christ has already been named, so that I do not build on someone else's foundation" (Romans 15:20).

Ferdinand Stahl was born in Michigan, in the United States of America, in January, 1874. At the age of 19, he married Ana Carlson, a migrant from Sweden. Nine years later, they were visited by an Adventist colporteur, and after study of the Bible, they decided to keep the Sabbath and join the Seventh-day Adventist Church.[1]

Their hearts were set on mission service, and they chose to study nursing in preparation for their work. After completing the nursing course at Battle Creek Sanitarium, they worked for a time in Ohio, then wondered in which distant land God would have them serve.

The decision was important enough for Ferdinand to write about it to Ellen White. He confided that they would like to work in "the most difficult place in the world"—perhaps Madagascar or with the Inca Indians in South America. She advised them to go to a General Conference congress in Washington in May–June, 1909, where they could meet Adventist leaders from around the globe. By the end of June, they were on their way to Peru, Bolivia and Lake Titicaca!

Within a short time, they had set up clinics, organised schools, were teaching the people to live healthfully and had arranged for baptisms. Ferdinand was said not to be a great public speaker. However, he was a wonderful teller of stories and the Indians loved to listen to him. He had a special approach which won many hearts. He went as a friend to the homes of the rich and the poor, greeting them with a Latin American hug, sometimes lifting them off their feet. He was happy to sit with them on the floor of their huts to enjoy a simple meal together. At times, he would sleep overnight as a member of the family. They would talk together about their children and the problems they were facing. They would pray together and he would give them medicine as they needed it.

The results were exciting. While Ferdinand Stahl was president of the Lake Titicaca Mission, there were 46 missionary schools operating, baptisms reached 500 in one year and the membership reached 2075. Ferdinand was called the "apostle of the indigenous."[2]

In 1939, 30 years after their arrival in Peru, Ferdinand's health was failing and the intrepid couple were persuaded to return to their homeland. He told of his work in the South American Highlands in a book titled *In the Land of the Incas*. In his book, he called for the young people of the church to "abandon their worldly ambitions and consecrate their lives to God, going to these needy fields, among people who have never heard the beautiful story of the cross." He also called on those who could not go out in this way to "give generously the resources entrusted to them" so that the work could be continued among "these children of Christ who are in darkness."

How wonderful to have the whole world open to us for work as Adventist teachers! What can we learn from Ferdinand and Ana Stahl about what to look for in choosing our next place to serve? Are there other important factors we should consider?

---

1 The story told here of Ferdinand and Ana Stahl is taken from Gluder Quispe, "Stahl, Ferdinand Anthony (1874–1950)," *Encyclopedia of Seventh-day Adventists* <https://encyclopedia.adventist.org/article?id=EGPP> and from Bent Axel Larsen, *Anna and Bent: Adventurers for God* (Mountain View, CA: Pacific Press Publishing Association, 1979).

2 Indigenous people are the earliest inhabitants of a region.

From enemy to ally

"Do not be afraid of them, for I am with you to deliver you, says the Lord" (Jeremiah 1:8).

In their travels up the Ucayali River in Peru, Ferdinand and Ana Stahl were begged again and again to send teachers to help the people in their need. At times, they were told that land had been set aside and that a schoolhouse was already built and waiting. The Stahls had set up a mission at Iquitos, so they decided to move there from Lima, the capital, as soon as they could sell their home.

A month went by and no-one came to look at their house. Then one afternoon, Ferdinand announced that he could not go out, for he needed to be there when the buyer arrived.

Ana asked, "How can you be so sure that a buyer will be coming?"

Ferdinand replied, "God hears prayers. He will send a buyer."

Sure enough a ship's captain called by and agreed to take the house and the furniture.

One evening after they were settled at the mission station, Ferdinand was preparing to hold worship in their small chapel by the river. Just then, two friendly Indians rushed into the compound with an urgent message for the pastor.

"Señor Stahl,"[1] one of them exclaimed, "Chief Huari is coming tonight to kill you. He is a witchdoctor. I heard him swear that he will kill you before you tell your strange story and use your miracle medicine in his village. He has already come down the river and hidden his canoe near here."

"After worship," said Ferdinand, "we will go and see him."

"Be careful," warned one of the visitors. "He can be very dangerous."

For worship that evening, Pastor Stahl read Jeremiah 1:8, "Do not be afraid of them, for I am with you to deliver you, says the Lord."

Then he prayed for God's protection and for the changing of the heart of the chief.

"Please wait until the morning," begged Ana. "He may hit you with one of his poison arrows."

"No," Ferdinand insisted. "We must find him and talk with him before he continues with his evil deed. We may save him and through him make friends with his people. God will be with us."

With one of the men from the mission and a flashlight, he set out along the riverbank. There was no sleep that night at the mission station, but much anxiety and prayer.

As the new day dawned, a cry went up, "Here they come!" Sure enough, there they were—the two mission men and a third man smiling broadly, with Ferdinand's arm around his shoulders. Pastor Stahl introduced his wife and then announced, "This is my new friend, Chief Huari."

After they shook hands, Ferdinand explained why they had been away so long—because Huari had hidden himself so well, it had taken some hours to find him. "Then," he explained, "we sat on the bank of the river in the moonlight and talked about the God who made all things and who loves us dearly. Chief Huari was angry at first, but then he began to listen to the Spirit of the Lord. Now, instead of an enemy, we have a good friend. In his heart, he has turned to Jesus, the Prince of Peace."

At this, with Ferdinand's arm still around him, Huari smiled broadly. He stayed at the mission station for several more days and then he returned happily to tell his own people what he had learnt.

In both our personal lives and in our teaching work we are likely to find those who resent us. How shall we regard them, approach them and speak with them so that the Spirit of God can best soften their hearts and turn them into friends who are ready to listen to what we have to say?

---

1 "Señor" (seen-your) is a polite title for a man in a Spanish-speaking culture—like Sir or Mister in English. Feminine equivalents are "Señora" (sen-your-uh) for a married woman, and "Señorita" (sen-yuh-ree-tuh) for an unmarried woman.

Believing is seeing

"A leper came to him begging him, and kneeling he said to him, 'If you choose, you can make me clean.' Moved with pity, Jesus stretched out his hand and touched him, and said to him, 'I do choose. Be made clean!'" (Mark 1:40, 41).

"[A spirit that causes dumbness] has often cast [my son] into the fire and into the water, to destroy him; but if you are able to do anything, have pity on us and help us.' Jesus said to him, 'If you are able!—All things can be done for the one who believes.' Immediately the father of the child cried out, 'I believe; help my unbelief!'" (Mark 9:22–24).

We have seen that Pastor Ferdinand Stahl, apostle to the indigenous people of Peru, had wonderful faith and that he lived according to that faith. Suppose my faith does not reach as high as his—dare I come seeking answers to prayer? Here are two events in the life of Jesus that may help us with that question.

The first occasion is from Mark 1 and is given above. We read of a man stricken with leprosy, the most dreaded disease in Palestine. He heard of a Healer who was going about Galilee teaching good news of deliverance and casting out demons. He might have watched from a distance and heard the assurance in Jesus' voice. Perhaps he was gripped by a conviction that this Healer could meet his need.

Breaking all the rules, he hurried over and knelt within arm's reach of Jesus. There he spoke from his heart to One who had power to meet the needs of every child on the planet: "If you choose, you can make me clean."

It was enough. The hand that upholds the galaxies in their motion reached out and touched the diseased body. The voice that originally called light and space into existence pronounced, "I do choose. Be made clean!"

The one-time leper could now join in joyful fellowship with God's family on earth and look forward to banqueting at the marriage supper of the Lamb.

The second event is from Mark 9 and also involves a plea for healing. Jesus, with Peter, James and John, had been on the Mount of Transfiguration overnight. There, the past glories of Israel had been brought to mind, with the presence of Moses, the great Hebrew law-giver, and Elijah, the first among the prophets—both descended from heaven to meet with Jesus. Soon a cloud had overshadowed the scene and the voice of God had been heard, "This is my Son, the Beloved; listen to him!" (Mark 9:7).

In the morning, Jesus and the three disciples were back on the plain below with the sights and the sounds of the heavenly kingdom still dazzling their senses. They came upon a sorry scene. A distraught father had come in search of Jesus for the healing of his epileptic son. In Jesus' absence, the nine disciples had tried and failed to cure the boy. They were then harassed by a group of Jewish experts in the law, quite likely taunting the disciples with their ineffectiveness. Jesus was the father's only hope, and He was seen approaching.

Soon the father took centre stage. He recited the sad situation of the boy and he begged, "If you are able to do anything, have pity on us and help us."

Jesus surely longed to heal the boy; however, there is something that can prevent a personal miracle—that is, the unbelief of those who seek it.[1] Would the father's doubts cut the boy off from healing?

Then Jesus echoed the words of the father, saying, "If you are able!" It was as if Jesus was asking the father if he was unsure whether he was talking to the divine Healer. Jesus added, "All things can be done for the one who believes."

Now the father could see that his own unbelief might prevent the healing of his child, and immediately he cried out through his tears, "I believe; help my unbelief!"

Was that enough? It was enough. The miracle took place.

What then are the differences and the similarities between the two occasions? One seeker had total assurance about what Jesus was able to do, while the other seemed to be unsure. In the end, the second asked for a miracle for himself—that his unbelief might be lifted into belief—as well as healing for his child. He learnt that anyone who comes to Jesus will never be driven away.[2]

In our country church, it was time for the study of the senior Sabbath school lesson, and there were seven or eight of us seated around a table in the church hall. The subject that week had been Daniel 10, following on from Daniel's important prayer in Chapter 9. We learnt how Michael and one of the angels had struggled against forces of evil that were clouding the mind of Cyrus, king of Persia, so that he would not let the Hebrew captives return to their homeland. After a long struggle, the evil powers were driven away, and Cyrus could think clearly and freely choose to set the captives free.

At that stage in our group study, a grandmother spoke about how she had previously prayed that God would change the minds of some of her family members so they would accept Jesus into their lives. Then, she said, it came to her that she should not ask for that, since God has made us all free to choose for ourselves the way we wish to think and act. After that, she was planning to pray that the evil forces surrounding the members of her family would be driven away, allowing each one to choose differently about spiritual things.

Are there students in our classes for whom we could pray in this way? We might also plan ways to turn their minds to positive influences, for example discovering their interests and offering some suitable reading or viewing material.

---

1 See Mark 6:4–6.

2 See John 6:37.

The indispensable church steeple

"You are the salt of the earth…the light of the world" (Matthew 5:13, 14).

Century after century, a church had stood high on a headland on the east coast of England. With its steeple pointing to the heavens, it was visible for miles around. It could also be seen from far out in the North Sea.[1]

Then there came a stormy night with high winds. At daylight, the vicar went out and came upon a dismal sight. He found the church steeple lying in pieces among the headstones in the churchyard. He returned indoors with a heavy heart.

Later that day, insistent knocking called him to find two well-dressed middle-aged men at his front door. Once seated in the living room, they came promptly to the reason for their visit.

"It's about your church steeple," they explained. "Are you planning to have it repaired? And soon?"

"It could take some months to raise the money," the vicar pointed out. "Why do you ask?"

"We are from the British Admiralty," they explained, "and are concerned for the safety of the ships going up and down this coastline. Your church and its steeple are on all the maps of this part of the east coast. For a century and more, mariners have been plotting their courses by reference to your steeple. Without it, ships could be in danger and lives lost."

The vicar nodded his understanding but replied, "I have no quick solution."

"In that case," responded one of the visitors, "the Admiralty will fund the repair. And we shall commence immediately."

There are important reminders in a story like this. Some things should never be allowed to fall into disrepair—like our relationship with God, the values we hold and the hope we share.

As well, we have an ever-present responsibility to maintain a clear vision of the original purpose and objectives of the Adventist system of church schools. Set up under God's leading, like the church steeple in our story, its goals must be kept standing to show the way forward.

The church and its steeple in today's reading were urgently needed as a secure point from which the course of ships in the North Sea could be plotted. Similarly, there might be secular institutions in our school districts that could be interested to learn something of the values cherished in a Christ-centred approach to education. Shall we be ready, at the same time, to learn of the ideals held by other school systems?

Come to think of it, how ready would we be to take a turn (at, say, a regional meeting) at sharing our philosophical ideals with teachers from other school systems? If this could be carried out winsomely, surely the "salt" will commence to add its distinctive flavour to the world around us and the "light" to show something of a new way.

What means could be open to us for meeting socially and informally with teachers from other schools, hearing about the challenges they are facing, sharing some of our own, and discussing promising ways ahead? In addition, are there educational bodies—such as curriculum committees, textbook advisory groups or taskforces for recommending student learning outcomes—that could be a forum for this type of interchange?

---

1 The present writer has a clear recollection of coming upon the story of the fallen church steeple in a second-hand bookshop in Sydney, something like 50 years ago. I did not buy the book, nor do I recall its title; however, I believe it was written by the notable American pastor, Harry Emerson Fosdick (1878–1969). The anecdote has been adapted here from memory.

Answered prayers in Uganda

"I will rebuke the devourer for your sakes, and he shall not destroy the fruits of your ground" (Malachi 3:11, KJV).

Magdalon Lind[1] was baptised with his mother in Norway in the year 1926. The following year, he decided to go to the Norwegian Adventist Junior College at Onsrud, near Jessheim. This would give him time to think about his life work. He was good at soccer: perhaps he should be a professional footballer—or maybe a ship's officer? It's not easy to choose when you are only 16 years old and there are so many possibilities.

Several things happened that year that pointed his life in new direction. First, he met an attractive young woman, also 16 years of age, who was taking some of the same classes as he. Her name was Kezia Sørbøe.[2] On both sides, it was love at first sight. Both of them came to believe that they should prepare to be missionaries in a foreign country.[3]

For training, Kezia went to the Adventist sanitarium at Skodsborg in Denmark, where she studied nursing and physical therapy. Magdalon went to Newbold College in England to study theology. Later, Kezia joined him there and studied to improve her English.

While they were still in England, they were asked by the president of the Northern European Division[4] to visit him in his office. In the course of the conversation, he asked if they were vegetarians. They were not and they told him so, wondering if this would stand against their being appointed to a mission field. As it turned out, the president was relieved, and told them it could be hard for vegetarians in parts of Africa, where he would like to call them as missionaries.

An Adventist nurse had died there trying to live on beans and potatoes.

With their studies complete, Magdalon and Kezia were back in Norway, where they were married among their families and friends on June 1, 1935. Their honeymoon was spent on board a German ship, which took them via the Mediterranean Sea and the Suez Canal to Kenya. There, they took a train to Uganda, where they were to serve for 20 years.

The Linds' first mission station was at Nchwang. A dispensary was set up at once, and on the first day, they found a long line of villagers waiting for help. Kezia gave all the medical help she could and Magdalon went out into "the bush" to meet as many of the people as possible. They loved his enthusiasm and friendliness and enjoyed his Bible stories. Later, the hearers told his stories to others, and it became difficult to keep up with the calls to set up mission work in new areas.

After one year, they were asked to take charge of the Kakora Mission Station in the Eastern Province of Uganda. An early project was the building of a larger school. Magdalon and the schoolboys formed the bricks in wooden moulds, and when they had dried out, they had them burnt. In this way, they built three classrooms and an office. There was room for both the children and their parents, with all excited to learn to read. In the afternoons, the boys joined happily with Magdalon in playing soccer.

Later, they moved to Mitandi, near the famous "Mountains of the Moon." Seeing the need there, they started a junior school and the young people flocked in. From that school, an army of workers emerged. Many went on to train as pastors, teachers and health workers. A number went on to become church leaders and university professors.

A young man called Kindakenda was given work at the mission station before he started his schooling. One morning, he did not arrive and a message was sent to say he was sick. A few days later, there was still no sight of him, so Pastor Lind set out to call at his home. He was found lying in bed, thin and weak.

Soon, it was discovered that Kindakenda had been visited by a witchdoctor, who had placed a curse on him. He found parts of a chicken and some blood at the entrance to his home, which left him quite sure that he would soon die. And that was what was happening.

"Why didn't you tell me you had been cursed?" asked Pastor Lind. "I can help you. We will pray to our God and the witchdoctor will have no power over you. Then I will give you some medicine. You will sleep well tonight and feel much better tomorrow." He prayed and then gave Kindakenda a cup of water with aspirin and Epson salts. Sure enough, he was soon back at work.

On an earlier occasion, Magdalon and Kezia were outside just before harvest time on a Friday afternoon, preparing for Sabbath. Suddenly, the sky became quite dark and they wondered if there was going to be a storm. The African villagers knew better—this was a swarm of millions of locusts. If they were to settle, their crops would be eaten to bare earth and they would be faced with famine. Hoping to drive the locusts away, they commenced to shout and beat on anything they could find to make a noise. It was no use.

Pastor Lind urgently called those within hearing of his voice to gather for prayer. They stood with bowed heads as he asked God for deliverance. He referred to Malachi 3:11, where God promised to "rebuke the devourer" and protect "the fruits of your ground."

When they raised their heads, they saw the swarm turning and making its way out of sight. They looked at each other with tear-filled eyes and then gave thanks to God for the loving care they had received.

There are different kinds of answers people can give when we make a request. These can include: Yes, No, and Not just now. Answers to prayers may also be of different kinds. For example, the apostle Paul had a particular bodily ailment that was a worry to him in his service for God. Three times, he prayed that it would be taken away (see 2 Corinthians 12:7–10). However, rather than take it away, God chose to give him strength to bear it and carry on. In this way, he became an example to us all. We know, as well, that John the Baptist was imprisoned. We can be confident that many prayed that he might be released. In the end, his life was taken there in the dungeon, but he was given the assurance that Jesus was the Messiah and that his life was in God's hands (see Matthew 14:3–12.)

With our reading for today in mind, together with the above stories from the Bible, what principles can we follow in making requests to God in prayer for ourselves, our work and our students? What other Bible principles can guide us?

---

1 His first name is pronounced "MAG-duh-lon."

2 In English, the pronunciation is "KEE-zee-uh SUHR-buh."

3 Sources for the present reading and the next are Kezia Lind, *Africa Called Us* (Sandefjord, Norway: Publisher, 2013); and Yona Balyage, Nathaniel Mumbere Walemba, "Lind, Magdalon Eugen (1910–1985) and Kezia (1909–2013)," in *Encyclopedia of Seventh-day Adventists* <https://encyclopedia.adventist.org/article?id=AFD9>.

4 At that time, the Northern European Division included British East Africa.

A surprise letter and a well-informed stranger

"Before they call I will answer, while they are yet speaking I will hear" (Isaiah 65:24).

Meri Kahinju was a widow and she attended a Christian church with her bright 12-year-old son, Absalom. They lived at Kazingo, near Fort Portal, west of Kampala, Uganda. One night, in a dream, she saw a European and heard a voice say, "You must go and hear this man."

Soon after, Meri, Absalom and several of her friends made their way to the village meeting place to listen to a man who had come to talk about God. They watched as the speaker went forward to begin preaching. Leaning over to her friends, she whispered, "That is the man I saw." It was Pastor Magdalon Lind from Norway.

Each day, Meri and Absalom returned and heard the stories and Bible messages that Adventists love to share. They were baptised soon after. Meri knew that her son was bright and that he should attend school. However, she could not afford the school fees. She and Absalom visited Pastor Lind and told him about it. He explained that the Adventist school at Kazingo was short of money and there were no further free places. They prayed together, and as she prepared to leave for home, he said they would do what they could.

Only a few minutes earlier, the mail boy had returned from town on his bicycle. One of the letters was from the United States and had been posted two months before. Magdalon opened it and discovered it was from an Adventist who knew a man who had earlier lived in

Uganda. He read, "If there is a boy or girl who wants an education and has no money, and if you consider them worthy to be paid for, I would like to help them."

Pastor Lind hurried outside and called to Meri and Absalom to return. He read the letter to them and they thanked God that it had arrived the day it was needed, after being on its way all those weeks. Absalom attended school and did well. He went on to train as a teacher, and later became the principal of an Adventist school in the Toro Province.

During Magdalon and Kezia's first furlough back to Norway, Nazi Germany commenced warfare in Europe. In January, 1940, they needed to return to Uganda with their two small girls, both under four years old. They could travel all the way by ship, across the North Sea and through the Mediterranean. However, ships had already been torpedoed in the North Sea, so they set out to go by train across Germany,[1] planning to stay overnight in Berlin before continuing on to Italy where they could take a ship for the Suez Canal.

As they approached the city in the darkness, a stranger came into their train compartment and sat down next to Pastor Lind. To his surprise, the newcomer began to ask a number of questions in English. These included where they were going, whether they could speak German, where they were staying, and whether they had a torch. Magdalon told him they were planning to take a taxi from the station to a nearby hotel.

The stranger seemed to be concerned. He explained that there were no taxis or streetlights due to the war. He offered to help them get to some accommodation fairly close by. Magdalon went out into the corridor where Kezia was with one of the children and explained the situation to her. "Can we trust him?" she asked. However, they had no other choice and decided to accept his help.

It was almost midnight when they arrived at the platform. They climbed out and stood in the chill of a midwinter night. The stranger led the way, holding a torch. Finally, after a change of trains and several flights of stairs, they came out onto the street, crossed over to a hotel and followed the man up into the lobby.

He seemed to know exactly what to do. He approached the desk and spoke with authority to the clerk, "This family has been travelling all day and needs a room and a meal."

"I'm sorry," explained the clerk, "we have nothing available."

"No," replied the stranger, "Room 701 is vacant."

After a quick check, the clerk replied, "Yes, the people who were in there have moved out without my knowing. You can have that room."

Further explanation was given regarding a meal for that night, breakfast in the morning and assistance in boarding the train for the next section of their journey. It was all just what they needed. Remembering himself, Magdalon turned to shake the stranger's hand and thank him for his kindness. To his amazement, their helper had vanished—there was no-one in sight. It was a reminder that God's children need never walk alone.

Back in British East Africa, having travelled through Germany, Magdalon and Kezia were under suspicion as acting as German spies. Finally, they were accepted as safe residents, and two officers of the British army asked them if Bible prophecy tells us if Hitler would come to control Europe. They were glad to hear from Magdalon that this was not going to happen.[2]

Have members of the staff had an instance when they believe they were specially cared for by an unknown helper? Here is one such occasion when the present writer had something like this happen.

I was a young teacher in my early 20s and making my way home from church school on a motor scooter in the early evening. I chose what had always been a quiet route; it involved crossing a narrow bridge that allowed for one lane of traffic in each direction, with a raised footpath on the outer edges of the bridge. As I entered the bridge, a small plumber's truck did the same, travelling in the opposite direction. At the crest of the bridge, the vehicle suddenly swerved into my lane and came directly at me. The only choice I had was to apply the hand brake and lurch my motor scooter up onto the raised sidewalk.

It soon became apparent that the action of the truck driver had saved my life. Without my noticing it in the fading light, a length of steel piping had shaken loose from the bed of the truck and come to rest with a metre or so extending across my laneway. If either vehicle had continued normally, I would have been struck across the chest and thrown onto the road.

Incredibly, within a split second, the truck driver had caught sight of the displaced piping, had decided there was no time to brake, and had aimed the vehicle onto my side of the roadway to force me to mount the sidewalk. I am willing to believe he was prompted by an unseen protector.

I was thankful for the outcome—and still am today.

---

1 Since Magdalon and Kezia were Norwegians and not British, they were allowed 48 hours to cross Germany and make the trip to Italy.

2 Pastor Magdalon Lind went on to hold a number of leading positions in the Seventh-day Adventist Church. In 1960, he was appointed president of the East African Union, then as executive secretary of the Trans-Africa Division in 1965. In 1970, he became president of the newly organised Afro-Mideast Division centred in Beirut, Lebanon, with responsibility for Uganda, Kenya, Ethiopia, Tanzania and the Middle East. Magdalon and Kezia finally retired back in Norway. Magdalon lived until March 25, 1985, age 74, and Kezia until July 24, 2013, age 103.

Building rapport

"Those who are wise shall shine like the brightness of the sky, and those who lead many to righteousness, like the stars forever and ever." (Daniel 12:3).

Dorothy Minchin spent much of her childhood in Singapore, where her parents served as missionaries for several years before World War II.[1]

In the closing months of 1941, the family took furlough in Australia, her father's homeland. So it was that Dorothy, at 12 years of age, found herself standing in line with the secondary school beginners at the Avondale Central School the next year.[2] The students were all in school uniform—a grey tunic and black stockings for the girls. In spite of this, she felt shy, awkward and dreadfully out of place.

Dorothy turned her attention to the line-up of teachers standing along the school verandah, hoping to find a sense of security from them. The first thing she noticed was their youthfulness. When one of them was introduced, she felt a buzz of enthusiasm from those around her. It was Robert Parr, 21 years old and several years out of teacher training at the nearby Avondale College. He was introduced as Mr Parr, and the newcomer from Singapore soon discovered he was to be her Latin teacher.

And such classes they were! Writing of them 23 years later, Dorothy Minchin Comm remembered the fun that was unleashed, together with a quiet dignity and enthusiastic commitment to learning. Amid the spontaneous bursts of laughter he prompted, she learnt to recite the various declensions of Latin nouns and to find Caesar's Gallic Wars as riveting as the war then raging in the nearby Pacific. Sensing Mr Parr's approval was like basking in a ray of sunshine, and in Latin classes her uneasiness seemed to evaporate.

Some weeks after school began, Dorothy faced what was to her a double calamity—her favourite teacher had cause to give her an after-school detention. And just as bad, he was to be the supervising teacher. When the lines he had set her to write were complete, she took them with great embarrassment to Mr Parr, who was seated at the desk at the front of the room.

After looking them over, he remarked on the misdemeanor that had earned the detention: "You were a bit of a chump to do that, weren't you?" Speechless with misery, she nodded. Then with a confiding smile and perhaps an upward flicker of the eyebrows, he added, "I say, you don't mind my calling you a chump when you *are* one, do you?" She agreed with a shy smile of her own.

Writing of the occasion years later, the adult Dorothy—by then a teacher herself in the West Indies—noted, "By some subtle magic known to comparatively few teachers, rapport had been established again."[3]

What might have been the secret behind Robert Parr's rapport with the students he taught? What do you notice about the way he combined discipline and humour?

---

1 This story is adapted from Dorothy Minchin Comm, "His Name is Parr," *The Youth's Instructor*, April 27, 1965, pages 9, 10.

2 In Australian schools, primary school grades generally finish at the close of Year 6. Secondary classes commence with Year 7 and go on to Year 12.

3 Rapport (pronounced "RAP-or") is a relationship where people understand each other and are able to communicate happily. Teachers are pleased to have rapport with whole classes.

A friend in need

"Whoever becomes humble like this child is the greatest in the kingdom of heaven. Whoever welcomes one such child in my name welcomes me" (Matthew 18:4, 5).

With years of teaching now behind him, Robert Parr worked for a time in a non-Adventist secondary school. One of his duties was giving struggling students a series of tests to discover the reasons for their problems. This was followed by suitable catch-up work to help them meet the standard of their class.[1]

After classes, on a day of torrential rain, Robert was sitting at his desk correcting a student assignment. Without warning, a lad arrived at his door wearing a dripping raincoat, with a pair of thin, knobbly legs showing beneath it. A smile and an upward tilt of the head prompted the boy to come to the desk and introduce himself: "I'm Albert K, sir,"[2] he said. "The principal said to come to see you, and you would give me 'the works.'"

That meant a full range of tests, starting with one for measuring intelligence. An appointment was made for a little later in the week. Meanwhile, Robert arranged to see the principal about the boy, and their discussion was quite revealing. It turned out that Albert's father was a well-known businessman in the city of Sydney and that his mother's photograph was to be seen from time to time on the social pages of one of the daily newspapers. Both parents, the principal confided, doted on their only child, showering him with gifts, pocket money, clothing and frequent holidays.

As Robert worked with Albert, he found him to be thoughtful, polite, unselfish and unaffected. It seemed that none of his parents' lavish attentions had spoiled the boy. Establishing rapport gave no trouble—the teacher saw it as "just making friends." In the process, he discovered that his young friend was fascinated by things that hop, wriggle, swim and fly. Albert frequently shared a sample of the specimens he was collecting.

And how the boy could work! Heavy assignments would be passed back promptly. When he was urged not to neglect the work given to him by other teachers, he would agree with, "Yes, sir, I'll do as you say." Then the following morning, he would arrive with a huge load of finished work, together perhaps with a spider in a screw-top jar, and pass it all over with a shy smile.

However, after several weeks, a problem arose from an unexpected source. One afternoon, Robert found a note on his desk with a phone number, asking that he call Albert's mother. She wanted to arrange an interview with him. They arranged a time, and she ended the call with: "I expect you will not like what I am going to say." Robert prepared himself for a difficult interview.

At the appointed time, there was a sharp *rat-tat* at his door, and in came Mrs K, with firm steps, a determined look in her eyes and pursed lips. Robert welcomed her and invited her to be seated. She quickly came to the point of her visit.

"It's about Albert," she said. "What is this nonsense about *diagnostic tests* and *remedial* help?"

He explained the situation and assured her that it should not be long before her son would be up with the rest of the class.

The visitor did not seem to hear. She went on, "Albert's father is a leading businessman in this city and we both have above-average intelligence, so by the laws of heredity, our son must be brilliant and well able to carry out the work of his class."

Robert tried again to give a word of encouragement. However, she was not finished, "You shame us in giving my son this baby-work. And you are destroying his confidence."

Her unkindest speech for the day was aimed at Robert himself. "Besides," she said, with a tilt of her head and narrowed eyelids, "my husband and I consider that if Albert ever does need coaching, it should be with an... *expert*." And there was much more.

He did not take the time to tell Mrs K of the many students he had helped to get back into their regular classwork. However, while she was catching her breath, he spoke rapidly of the program of assignments he had planned for Albert—work that he could manage well and that would give him increased confidence.

In the end, they reached a compromise. Albert would be allowed to do this extra homework once all his regular assignments were finished. After a limp handshake, Mrs K left the room, tight-lipped.

Just a few minutes later, Albert himself could be seen standing at the doorway. Robert nodded his head, smiled and said, "Come in."

Half way to the desk, he stopped, twitched his nostrils and asked, "Has my mother been to see you?"

"Yes, how did you know?"

"I could tell that perfume anywhere. What did she want?"

Robert explained that his mother was worried the catch-up assignments would hold up his regular subjects.

"But," said Albert, "this work is helping me with all my subjects. It's the best thing I've ever done. And I haven't missed any other assignments." Then he added with a shy smile, "I'm mighty grateful to you for all this, sir."

A lighter assignment than usual was passed over, together with the advice, "No hurry for this—just whenever you can."

"I'll do it tonight, sir," was the prompt reply.

And there it was on the desk on the following morning. No surprise in that. However, there was a shock in opening the assignment—it was a mess! The numbers were hardly recognisable. Instead of being ruled straight, the lines straggled up and down the page and there were smudges everywhere. How could the boy dare to hand in such a shocking performance?

When Albert appeared in the afternoon, he was spoken to sternly. "Albert," Robert said, "this work is dreadful. What is the meaning of this?"

Albert shuffled his feet, looking down before meeting Robert's eyes.

"I'm sorry it looks so bad, sir," he said. "I didn't want to let you down. Last night, as soon as I'd finished my other work, mother sent me straight off to bed—and made me leave the door open so she could see if the light was on.

"I took the assignment, a torch and a fountain pen into bed with me. Then I knelt up under the blankets to make a kind of tent. I did the work for you as well as I could. I'm sorry about the crooked lines and the smudges. Next time, sir, I'll do better—I'll take a ruler in with me and a ballpoint pen."

With eyes misting over, Robert looked again at the blots, smudges, wobbly figures and crooked lines. Were they a disgrace? Never. Never. They were shining stars witnessing to the self-forgetfulness, gratitude, affection and humility that can place these students of ours among the greatest in the kingdom of heaven.

Is anything further coming through with regard to Robert Parr's overall approach? Here was a teacher who understood the attitude of the students with whom he was working. Winning the student's confidence was foundational. Having "made friends," he went on to treat his students with consideration, courtesy and respect—but not with familiarity. Through it all, he continued to maintain acceptable standards and the "friendship" was always a relationship between a teacher and a student.

It is possible for such relationships to end up going the wrong way. In this regard, young teachers—and some not so young—have been known to come to grief, with their teaching work terminated and students' lives harmed. Some safeguards are suggested: When giving individual help to students, do so with others around you wherever possible and always with an open door. Refrain from physical contact. If a student writes a personal note to a teacher, get the school principal's advice on what to do. When with students, say and do only what you would say and do in the presence of their parents.

---

1 The story is adapted from R H Parr, "The GQ of Albert K.," *The Youth's Instructor*, May 31, 1960, pages 12–16.

2 Albert gave his family name; it is not mentioned here.

"There is therefore now no condemnation for those who are in Christ Jesus" (Romans 8:1).

"For all who are led by the Spirit of God are children of God" (Romans 8:14).

Thousands have followed the footsteps of Christian, a man dressed in rags, carrying a book and "a great burden." In imagination, they have watched him read from the book and cry out through his tears, "What shall I do?"[1]

The story of Christian's journey from the City of Destruction to the Celestial City is found in the book *Pilgrim's Progress*. Author John Bunyan started writing the book as a result of a dream, while he was in prison for holding church meetings separate from those arranged by the leading church of his day. His story was first published in 1678 and has been in print ever since.

Pilgrim's Progress is an allegory of the experiences modern Christians might face as we make our way to heaven.[2] In the story, the pilgrim comes upon a cross standing at a rise in the pathway. There, the burden on his back is loosed and tumbles away, never to be seen again. The sight of the cross and all that it means brings another flood of tears—this time not of fear but of joy and thankfulness.

Through his tears, Christian realises that three "Shining Ones" are standing beside him. One tells him, "Thy sins be forgiven thee." The second takes off his rags and gives him a new suit of clothes. The third sets a mark on his forehead and gives him a "roll"—a small scroll—with a seal on it, which he bids him to look at on his journey and eventually give in at the celestial gate.[3]

Allegories, of course, are meant to be unravelled. With the help of God's Word and God's Spirit, we are expected to discover the meaning of the people, places and items in the story. Some parts of the riddle are plainer than others. For example, in the allegory, the cross clearly represents Jesus' death on the cross of Calvary—that day of all days when, in unfailing love, "God was reconciling the world to himself in Christ, not counting people's sin's against them" and when Jesus was made "to be sin for us, so that in him we might become the righteousness of God" (2 Corinthians 5:19, 21, NIV).

The new suit of clothes given to Christian by one of the "Shining Ones" represents the gift of righteousness and the mark that was placed on his forehead represents Christian's recognition of Jesus' lordship in his life. That still leaves the scroll. What shall we make of it?

The scroll was to be looked at as Christian continued his pilgrimage. It was to be treasured in his bosom. It was "the assurance of his life" and the guarantee of his acceptance at the celestial gate.

The scroll is mentioned later in the story, when Christian is a guest at the Palace Beautiful. He is asked by Prudence, one of the maidens in attendance there, if his earlier way of life ever came back to his mind. He confesses that it is so and explains that such "inward and carnal cogitations" are now his grief. Prudence asks if he has experienced times times when those things "were vanquished."

In reply, Christian makes an unforgettable speech:

> Yes, when I think what I saw at the cross, *that will do it;* and when I look upon my broidered coat, *that will do it;* and when I look into the roll that I carry in my bosom, *that will do it;* and when my thoughts wax warm about whither I am going, *that will do it.*

I want to suggest that the scroll is related to the assurance God gives us in our texts for today. Am I choosing to be "in Christ Jesus," walking and living in the acceptance of His life and death for me? Then Romans 8:1 assures me that I will not be condemned.

Am I listening for the leading of the Spirit of God as I make plans and relate to those around me? Then, as Romans 8:14 promises, I am one of God's children—a member of His family.

If I feel discouraged or depressed, I may look into the "roll" that is kept in my "bosom"—at the Bible promises that assure me of God's mercy and acceptance. Better yet, I can memorise them so that they can be called to mind at any time. Regardless of how I feel, those passages are still true—and God will stand by them in dark times as well as in bright. They are there to be claimed and lived.

Our pilgrim walk need not be interrupted.

There may be some who claim to be within God's family while choosing to go against God's law—perhaps even in abusing others. What might be said about such a situation?

Since we are to examine ourselves, not others, shall we live by God's Word, accepting that it is those "who are led by the Spirit of God [who] are children of God" (Romans 8:14)?

---

1 The words are from the opening page of John Bunyan's *The Pilgrim's Progress*, Part One. The book was given special mention in Ellen White's *The Great Controversy* (page 252) as "hav[ing] guided many feet into the path of life."

2 An allegory is a story made up of symbols that represent things or ideas in real life.

3 This scene is from the section "Christian loses his burden," in John Bunyan's *Pilgrim's Progress*.

More beautiful than I

"Do nothing from selfish ambition or conceit, but in humility regard others as better than yourselves" (Philippians 2:3).

"[L]ove one another with mutual affection; outdo one another in showing honour" (Romans 12:10).

"[T]hrough love become slaves to one another" (Galatians 5:13).

"Be subject to one another out of reverence for Christ" (Ephesians 5:21)

When Christian first chose to flee his home in *Pilgrim's Progress*, he urged his wife and children to go with him; however, they would not listen. In the allegory, after her husband died, her thoughts were stirred in a new direction. She began to wonder if the way she had treated him had helped to cause his death.

One night, in a dream, she saw a large parchment, and on it was a record of her evil ways. While still asleep, she called out so loudly that her children heard, "Lord, have mercy upon me, a sinner!"

The following morning, a letter was delivered to her door—a message from the King, written in gold and inviting her to go on pilgrimage as her husband had done. Christiana (for that was her name) and her boys all determined to go. They were joined by a neighbour, a young woman called Mercy, who was welcomed by Christiana and told that the King "delighteth in Mercy."

After various adventures, they came to the Interpreter's House and there they had sweet fellowship and enjoyed bountiful assurance of God's love. After the evening meal, they retired to their rooms. There, Mercy thought constantly of the joy of her acceptance by God so that "now her doubts of missing at last were removed further from her than ever they were before."

In the morning, after they had bathed, the Interpreter called for the seal and applied it to their foreheads between their eyes. They now appeared more beautiful than ever and could be known as God's children wherever they went.

One more gift awaited them before they continued on their way. Garments were brought out—"fine linen, white and clean." These they put on, and they had a wonderful effect. Because they could not see themselves, they exclaimed to each other, "You are more beautiful than I am." Their words did not come from envy or vanity. Rather, they were humbly regarding others as better than themselves, as Paul counselled in Philippians 2:13.

What can we understand from the text: "Be subject to one another out of reverence for Christ" (Ephesians 5:21)?

It is interesting that while Paul spoke strongly against rivalry and conceit, there was one instance where he encouraged God's children to "outdo one another"—that is, in showing honour to others (Romans 12:10). As teachers, shall we take the opportunity to put this instruction into practice with comments to each other like these, perhaps during staff worship?

> *"That went really well."*
>
> *"I was watching the students as you were speaking in Assembly. It was really getting across to them."*
>
> *"You've been given a real gift for leading music and singing, and it's doing us all good!"*
>
> *"I couldn't help noticing in sports time yesterday afternoon how the game brought the kids from both teams close to each other. Individuals complimented each other and thanked each other for the compliments! I believe this is thanks to the atmosphere encouraged by our sports teachers."*

Passion that persists

"[Y]our young…shall see visions, and your old…shall dream dreams" (Acts 2:17).

Michelangelo Buonarroti (1475–1564) was a young man with a vision, and part of that vision was to sculpt a statue of David, the shepherd of Bethlehem. It was to be unlike any other *David* already on view—and he had seen his share of those in his native city of Florence, Italy.

The work was commenced in September, 1501, on a huge 5-metre (17-foot) chunk of Carrara marble.[1] The sculptor was a youthful 26 years of age—young enough to feel the pulse of idealism surging through his veins and to believe he could achieve something worthwhile. As the statue emerged from the splintering chips and scattering particles, it was commonly called "the giant." It was seen as representing the side of goodness and truth in the struggle with evil. So intent was the young artist on his project that he had stretches when he went without food and took snatches of sleep in his clothes.

The figure has its weight on the right leg and is turning to glare at the oncoming, boastful bully. The left hand holds the end of the sling draped over the shoulder, while the other hand, veins standing out prominently, has a firm grip on the missile that is to lay the assailant on his face. Cold, hard stone never looked more true to life.

Having bequeathed to humanity what might be the world's most famous piece of sculpture, Michelangelo faced another challenge nine years later. He was to chisel out not a teenage hero at the height of his vitality, but the 80-year-old Moses, who had been facing the management of an unruly pack of former slaves day after day. The result may be seen today in the church of San Pietro Vincoli in Rome.

Now 38 years of age, the sculptor introduces Moses to us as a man of dignity, purpose and authority. He is seated, we may assume, part way down the slopes of Mount Sinai. The tables of stone are under his right arm and the fingers of his right hand are threaded through the tresses of a richly flowing beard. The left arm is laid across his thighs with the index finger drawing our eyes to the Ten Commandments, which have recently been given to him by God on the mountain. His head is turned ominously to the left, perhaps having caught the sounds of idolatrous revelry around the golden calf on the plain below. His left leg is bent back as if he is about to stand and launch into the reform of his people.

A collection was made of 495 letters written by Michelangelo during his 89-year-long life. These were read carefully by biographer Irving Stone, who sought to better understand the sculptor and his works.[2] He noted, "David had been young, knowing he could conquer everything," whereas "Moses was ripe in years but with the inner strength to move mountains and form nations."[3]

Like Michelangelo and those ancient heroes, we—whether young or old—are called to make a lasting commitment. As we look to the future of our church school system, there are still inspirational visions to be captured by those youthful in years. There is still space for those who are older to dream with passion of the most effective paths ahead.

Those at the start of their teaching vocation might have already noticed things that might benefit from change—for example, teaching resources, methods, technology or organisation. Likewise, those who are older and more experienced may dream of a still more grand future for the church's school system than has yet been realised. Perhaps you have a passion for improving Bible curriculum for non-Christian students or ideas for reaching out to parents or stemming the haemorrhage of youth from the church. Is it time to share that dream with others, including school, conference and mission administrators?

---

1 Carrara is a city in the Tuscany region of Italy, northwest of Florence. It is famous for the beautiful marble that is taken from quarries in the nearby mountains.

2 Irving Stone, *The Agony and the Ecstasy* (New York: Penguin/Signet, 1987), page 759.

3 ibid, page 630.

No part is without importance

"It's like a man going away: He leaves his house and puts his servants in charge, *each with their assigned task*, and tells the one at the door to keep watch" (Mark 13:34, NIV).

The morning of Sunday, December 7, 1941, was tragic for the United States; a surprise attack was made by 353 Imperial Japanese war planes on American ships anchored in Pearl Harbor, Hawaii. Many of the United States' ships were lost or damaged, 188 planes were destroyed and 2403 servicemen were killed. Fear spread that the war was about to move further south.

In those days, most Adventist mission stations across the Pacific, with their clinics and schools, were managed by expatriate Australians. Pastor Norman Ferris had worked in the Marovo Lagoon area of the Solomon Islands for more than 20 years, and because of the war, he and his family were required to leave. The work there was left in the care of Solomon Islands pastor Kata Ragoso from 1942 to 1945.[1]

The mission in that area used three ships to carry out its work from island to island. These were MV *G F Jones*, MV *Dadavata*, and MV *Portal*[2]—all dear to the national crewmen who faithfully sailed them and to the Adventist mission community who often saw them leave to take the gospel to the surrounding islands. With war at their doorstep, these ships were taken over by the British army and were used to stop enemy patrols from entering the lagoon.

In 1942, the Japanese Imperial navy was so close that the British major knew he must leave. The engines on the *G F Jones* and *Dadavata* were started promptly. However, the *Portal* was older and needed a blowtorch to heat up the cylinder head. Since there was no time for that, the major gave the order for the ship to be destroyed so that it could not be used by the enemy. He had the ship doused in engine fuel, then took some cotton waste, lit it and threw it on board. After that, he left, with the two other ships under his control.

Pastor Ragoso and some of his fellow workers watched sadly from the beach as the *Portal* was engulfed in flames. This was God's boat and they wanted it to be kept safely for further gospel work. Together, they prayed that God would intervene. Then as they watched, the flames were suddenly stayed from one end of the *Portal* to the other.

With the enemy just a short distance away, the mission team knew they must act quickly. Canoes were brought out and lines were fastened to the prow of the *Portal*. Some worked with poles to guide the ship along a small creek flowing through the mangroves at the water's edge. All night they toiled. The masts were taken down. The ropes that were not burnt were untied. Palm fronds were cut and placed over the deck. By morning, the ship was well hidden.

Still they were not satisfied. What if the *Portal* were to be spotted? The engine must be made unusable. They brought screwdrivers and spanners, and the nuts and screws were removed one by one. The cylinder head was lifted off. Gaskets, tubes and springs were carefully removed.

What could be done with all the pieces? They were passed to the families living around the Marovo Lagoon, who were told to guard them with great care until they were called for. Some parts were hung from the trees. Some were wrapped and buried. Some were worn day by day: a young man had a belt with a row of nuts tied to it, and a young woman used some springs in her hair.

By May, 1945, the enemy had been driven from the Solomon Islands and the expatriate Australians were allowed to return to Marovo Lagoon to continue the work of the mission. Pastor Ferris arrived unexpectedly and was welcomed joyfully. He could see that Pastor Ragoso had led the mission work capably. Still, there was a lot of ground to be made up. Ships would be needed to visit near and distant villages, and he had been told by the British Admiralty that there wasn't one presently available. Even the *Portal,* they said, had been destroyed so the enemy couldn't use it.

When he told his news to the men from the village, they did not appear to be disheartened.

"*Portal* belongs to God," they said. "*Portal* did not burn. Wait and see."

And sure enough, within a day or so, they had the ship standing at the jetty. It looked bedraggled and needed a coat of paint. But the hull had no borers and was quite seaworthy. Pastor Ferris was pleased and excited. Then they came to the engine room.

"What is this? Half the engine is missing! And where can the parts be found?"

Again the villagers did not seem worried. Messengers were sent out around the lagoon: "Now is the time to bring in the parts of the engine!"

It had been almost three years since the pieces were passed to the members of the community. However, they began to arrive almost at once and they kept on coming as the days went by. There were large pieces that took two people to carry and there were pieces small enough to be carried in one hand. The engineers of the *Portal* started putting them together.

Every part was important. If a spring or a screw or a nut were missing, it could mean that the engine would not work. And it turned out that *there was not one piece missing*.

The next question was whether the engine could be started. Fuel was brought for the tank. Blowtorches were lit and applied to the cylinder head. A rope was given two turns around the flywheel and pulled vigorously. To the excitement of all present, the engine sprang to life and purred away as if it had been just yesterday that it was going about its regular work.[3]

Thanks to a faithful mission community, the *Portal* was on its way again as a vital means of gospel witness.

If the parts of the Portal *engine were to represent the staff of this present school (including those in a non-teaching role), what does this story suggest with regard to the relationship we have to each other?*

1 The present reading is adapted from Reuben E Hare, *Fuzzy Wuzzy Tales* (Washington, DC: Review and Herald Publishing Association, c.1950), pages 60–68; and Wilson Gia Liligeto, "Ragoso, Kata," in *Encyclopedia of Seventh-day Adventists* <https://encyclopedia.adventist.org/article?id=A836>.
Kata Ragoso is pronounced "KAH-Tuh RONG-Guh-Soh." The *Encyclopedia of Seventh-day Adventists* tells what the name means and how he came to be given it. See <https://encyclopedia.adventist.org/article?id=A836>.

2 The letters "MV" stand for "Motor Vessel." The ships had masts to carry sails and had engines as well.

3 Beside the cabin door on the *Portal* was a patch of partly burnt timber that the crew did not replace. This was to be a reminder of God's intervention on that exciting day in 1942.

"You've never known me!"

"God yearns jealously for the spirit that he has made to dwell in us.... Draw near to God, and he will draw near to you" (James 4:5, 8).

Frank Boreham (1871–1959), the oldest of 10 children, grew up in in a secure and happy home in the county of Kent, south-east of London. Later, he became a Baptist minister, serving in Mosgiel, New Zealand, and in Hobart and Melbourne, Australia. He read widely and he could write well—so well that his name was known around the world among other ministers.

He told a story of something that happened to him while he was still a lad.[1] An invitation came for him to visit the family of a friend for several days. On arrival, he was taken for a tour of the home. As they walked past a particular room, he was told that he must never go in there, and he obeyed the instruction faithfully. However, one day he happened to be passing that room and could not help but notice that the door was open. There was a bed on the opposite side of the room and in it was a boy close to his own age.

The young Frank paused in shock. He could see by the boy's face that he was hardly aware of what was going on around him. Then he saw the child's mother fall to her knees beside the bed. He heard her cry out in anguish, "I've fed you and clothed you and loved you—and you've never known me!"

Could there be many things more tragic for parents than that? By God's grace and an act of love, they brought into this world a living, breathing image of themselves—one with whom they looked forward to communing to the end of their days—and then discovered that it could never be.

Is our text for today telling us that God knows such anguish? In designing humans, He not only envisioned a collection of physical organs, not only the gift of reasoning, and the ability to make and enjoy things beautiful, God also gave us something that no other creature received—a "spirit to dwell in us," a spark of spiritual life that can reach out to God Himself. And we can get through too, if we reach out to Him. He waits, yearning to draw near to us, if only we are willing to draw near to Him.

When God watches over you and me jealously, not willing that we should choose another as our first love, does He ever say, "All this I gave you and did for you in love, yet you've never known Me"?

Our text for today points out that "God yearns jealously *for the spirit that He has made to dwell in us." The relationship between a husband and wife must not be shared with any other, and marriage partners have a right to guard that relationship jealously. Even more sacred is the relationship between God and His children, and He treasures it enough to guard it jeaously. Should we be surprised that God can have an attitude of jealousy? What is this telling us?*

---

1 This F W Boreham story is adapted here from William Barclay's version in *The Letter to the Romans*, Revised edition. (Philadelphia: The Westminster Press, 1975), page 124.

A legion of burning hearts

"Then God said, 'Let us make humankind in our image, according to our likeness'" (Genesis 1:26).

"[T]he Lord God formed man from the dust of the ground, and breathed into his nostrils the breath of life; and the man became a living being" (Genesis 2:8).

"Man, created for fellowship with God, can only in such fellowship find his real life and development. Created to find in God his highest joy, he can find in nothing else that which can quiet the cravings of the heart, can satisfy the hunger and thirst of the soul" (Ellen White, *Education*, page 124).

The intention of the Creation account in Genesis is unmistakable. All of God's creatures are important, but there is much that is special about humans. Our high destiny—to be made in the image of the Creator—was declared at first mention (see Genesis 1:26).[1] Then, in Genesis 2:7, we are told how the Creator shaped the dust of the ground and brought about a life-form unmentioned for any other part of the cosmos. To make the occasion still more momentous, the Lord God came close and imparted His own breath to His human child.

Here now was a "living being" with whom the Lord God could fellowship in some exciting ways. Ideas could be shared mind-to-mind—intellectually and logically. Moral choices—ideas of right and wrong—could be relayed and understood between them. Both alike could enjoy beauty, whether in sight or sound or touch. Both could delight in creating that which is lovely.

Humans were given a far-reaching freedom. Made to enjoy loving fellowship with our Creator, we were free to accept and return that love or to refuse it—to stay by our Maker or to turn our backs on Him. Is there any other love worthy of the name, even though allowing freedom to rebel opens up a great risk?

Many of God's creatures have senses that bring the planet and its unnumbered excitements within their reach. Some of those creatures have senses more spectacular than our own five: sight, hearing, smell, taste and touch. However, God's "likeness-children" can also experience reality through a sixth sense: the spirit. The possession of this gift from God is among our highest claims to nobility.

It is clear that not all of our human brothers and sisters exercise this spiritual sense to the same extent. Let me illustrate.

Long ago, at God's bidding, 12 apparently dry staffs were placed in the wilderness tabernacle by Moses.[2] The following day, they were brought out and examined. Eleven of the staffs came out no different from the way they had gone in. However, while in the sanctuary, one of the staffs "put forth buds, produced blossoms and bore ripe almonds" (Numbers 17:8).

There is something for us to learn here. We too go into sacred places from time to time. We hear prayers offered for God to be present and for Him to speak to our hearts. We sit and listen to the reading of God's Word. Even so, like the 11 staffs, it is possible for us to go out no different from when we went in.

However, it need not be that way. We may yearn for God to speak to us and experience Him drawing near by His Spirit. We may come to understand Him as never before and realise our lives can never be the same again. Like Aaron's staff, we can bear fruit and live lives with exciting new hopes and goals and plans.

A beautiful story is told in the last chapter of Luke's gospel. Two grieving followers of Jesus were walking from Jerusalem to their home in the village of Emmaus. It was the third day after the crucifixion (by Jewish reckoning). As they walked, Jesus Himself joined them and went on to explain the scriptures concerning Himself. They did not recognise Him then, and only later when He blessed and broke the bread for the evening meal did they realise it was Jesus. Then "he vanished from their sight" (Luke 24:31).

Remembering the way He spoke to them on their journey, they exclaimed: "Were not our hearts burning within us . . . while he was opening the scriptures to us?" (Luke 24:32).

It is worth asking whether our own hearts have burnt within us through communion with our Creator, as we prepare to teach. When this happens, the fire may spread to those to whom we minister, through the prompting of God's Spirit. Then, with us, they may be part of the legion of burning hearts. Their heart cravings and soul hunger may be satisfied as never before.

What might take place in our classrooms that could prompt our young people to draw near to God?

---

1 A number of these points are well stated in Joseph Fichtner, *Man, the Image of God* (New York: Alba House, 1978), pages 34–38. For example, "The divine artist stylises man after himself" (page 34); "[man] must be oriented toward God to achieve his destiny" (page 36); "[Man's] spirit opens him to the supernatural" (page 37); and "To be self-fulfilling [man's] spirit has to reach out to God who alone knows the mystery of man and his needs" (page 38).

2 The story is told in Numbers 17:1–11.

The postmistress

"For we are God's handiwork, created in Christ Jesus to do good works, which God prepared in advance for us to do" (Ephesians 2:10, NIV).

In 1890, John Wanamaker, the new postmaster-general of the United States of America, assembled postmasters and postmistresses from across the country at Washington DC.[1] Over three days, they spoke of ways to improve the postal service. Communication was of immense national importance with 63 million Americans scattered unevenly from coast to coast.

For the final evening, Wanamaker arranged a banquet to celebrate their achievements. The president and the secretary of state were invited, and so was Kate Field, one of the best loved writers and actresses in the country. She accepted the invitation on the condition she would not be called upon to speak.

With the meal concluded, Wanamaker spoke approvingly of what had taken place over the previous three days, and congratulations were given by the president and the secretary of state. At this point, the postmaster-general was about to bring the events of the evening to a close. However, before he could do so, a chorus of voices was heard across the room: "Kate Field! Kate Field!"

Wanamaker leaned over and suggested to the actress that even a few words would be appreciated. While he was speaking with her, the clamour around the banquet hall became hushed. He looked up to see a small, plain country woman standing up in the middle of the room. She wore an outmoded bonnet, with a faded shawl draped across her shoulders.

Kate Field summed up the situation in moments. A glance at the list of guests showed that the postmistress from the fourth-class post office at Cumberland Corners, Kentucky, also went by the name of Kate Field. She realised there might soon be a further chorus of voices telling the backwoods woman to sit down.

Immediately, the actress rose from her chair, clapped her hands, and called: "Kate Field of Kentucky!" The crowd followed her example and the small, country woman commenced to speak.

"This is the last thing I expected. Why would you want *me* to speak? When I got the invitation, I didn't see how I could come at all—what with Ma not able to get out of her wheelchair—and who would look after the chickens and the young turkeys? But then, when you was callin' for me to speak, I was sayin' to myself that maybe you was wantin' to hear not just about the big post offices, but about the little ones like mine too.

"You know they tell jokes about us readin' the mail. For me that ain't no joke. Lots of the mountain folk don't come down but once a month. Mail seldom comes for them 'cept bad news like sickness or death. So, if mail comes, I reads it. Then I gits somebody with a sure-footed mule and a willin' heart to take it where it orter go.

"Oh yes, while I'm confessin' to you all, and specially to our postmaster-general, I once committed forgery. Widder Hover's boy, Jake, ups and runs away, and she had nary a word from him. Then one day a letter comes and I gits a message to her. She can't read a word, but she never lets on. She says, 'Kate, read it fur me; I'm havin' heaps of trouble with my eyes.'

"So I reads it to myself: 'Dear Ma, this is a fine country up north. I am well and I hope you are the same. I hope you can send me some money soon. I sure need it. Jake.'

"When I seed what it said, I pretended I'd haster git my glasses. So I stepped out o' sight and changed the last part to read: 'I hope I can send you some money soon. You sure need it.'

"If you had seen the widder's face, you'd been glad if you had committed forgery. She went out like she had wings and ashoutin', 'I knowed there was good in Jake.'

"And then I wrote that good-fur-nothin' a letter. I telled him how I committed forgery to save his face to his poor old ma. And I said,

'If you don't git to work and git some money and send it to your ma, I'm comin' up thar and, when I am through with you, you'll look funny runnin' aroun' with no skin on you.' And he did.

"I know readin' the mail is not in the rules of the department. But it's in my rules. It builds families and does good all around. We has to be a lot of things, postmistresses like me—doctor, nurse, confessor, an' lots else. But jes' listen to me. I didn't plan to go on like this. I'm only Kate Field, postmistress, Cumberland Corners, Kentucky, the best fourth-class post office in this good ol' USA."

Then she took her seat, and the applause was deafening, with everyone in the banquet room on their feet. When the applause had subsided, Wanamaker, with tears running down his face, announced, "Every newspaper man must see me here before leaving."

The postmaster-general let it be known that, in the reporting of the evening, no mention was to be made of the mistake the Kentucky postmistress had made. "We can't break such hearts as that," he added. "That part of the story must not be printed while she is living."

The years went by and the faithful postmistress at Cumberland Corners became more and more frail. Then came a morning when the door to the post office was not opened. When there was no answer to their knocking, one of the residents went in through an open window. She found Kate lying still and peaceful in bed, holding a piece clipped from a Washington newspaper, the last lines of which read:

> The closing speech was the speech of the evening. The ovation at its close should warm the speaker's heart till the end of her days.

Two words had been added in post office ink, in a trembly old hand: "It did."

What makes this impromptu speech by the country postmistress so moving? How might it be viewed in the light of our headline text for today? What do the story and this text have to tell us about our role as Christian teachers?

---

1 This story is adapted from Elmer E Helms, "Kate Field—Postmistress," *Australasian Record*, July 2, 1983. (No indication was given of the original source of the article.)

A final word

There were once two men who were placed in the lock-up overnight. The following morning, they were called in to face a hypocritical bunch of interrogators. The fearless response of the pair brought on a unanimous observation: "[T]hey took note that these men had been with Jesus" (Acts 4:13, NIV).

The two, of course, were the apostles, Peter and John. They had, indeed, been with Jesus. They had been with Him on the shores of Galilee, where they received their call. They had been with Him when He rebuked a raging storm into peaceful calm. They had been with Him when, as Master of the cosmos, He had made clear His authority over a legion of demons.

They had also been with Jesus when the resurrected Lord gave the gospel commision and proclaimed His hold on all power in heaven and on earth. They had heard His command to go in that power and make disciples of all nations. They treasured the promise that Jesus would be with them personally for all time.

Small wonder that people—good and bad—could not help noting that this fearless pair had been with the divine Teacher.

What of ourselves—we who have adopted the practice of "listening in the morning," both personally and as a band of committed teachers? May it be said of us that we too have "been with Jesus."

Acknowledgments

The suggestion for the writing of this collection of devotional readings came from Dr Carol Tasker, who was at the time education director for the South Pacific Division of the Seventh-day Adventist Church. In addition, she kindly agreed to read through and comment on early clusters of the emerging manuscript. It was Dr Tasker, as well, who suggested that readings concerning the general spirituality of maturing Christians be included, in addition to the classroom-related readings.

Special appreciation is expressed for the part played by Dr David McClintock, present education director for the South Pacific Division, in the progression of this work. He has read and commented on the readings and recommended the publication of the book to Signs Publishing. His counsel has always been valuable.

Encouragement for the project was also given by Dr Andrew Montero, education director for the East-Central Africa Division, and he and Professor Yona Balyage gave advice regarding resources related to early Adventist mission work in East Africa.

Appreciation is also expressed for the contribution of Dr Darius Jankiewicz, field and ministerial secretary for the South Pacific Division—in particular for his willingness to look over the theology in several selections from the book.

Finally, my thanks to the editorial team at the Signs Publishing Company—Nathan Brown and Lauren Webb—for the interest and enthusiasm they have shown for this project. It has been a pleasure and an inspiration to work with them both.

It should be noted, of course, that none of these folk is to be held responsible for the final product. The writer takes full responsibility in this regard.